LET'S PUT KIDS FIRST, FINALLY

Getting Class Size Right

CHARLES M. ACHILLES

CORWIN PRESS, INC.
A Sage Publications Company
Thousand Oaks, California

For information address:

Corwin Press, Inc.
A Sage Publications Company
2455 Teller Road
Thousand Oaks, California 91320
E-mail: order@corwinpress.com

SAGE Publications Ltd.
6 Bonhill Street
London EC2A 4PU
United Kingdom

SAGE Publications India Pvt. Ltd.
M-32 Market
Greater Kailash I
New Delhi 110 048 India

Printed in the United States of America

Library of Congress Cataloging-in-Publication Data

Achilles, Charles M.
  Let's put kids first, finally : Getting class size right /
Charles M. Achilles.
    p. cm.
 Includes bibliographical references and index.
 ISBN 0-8039-6806-X (cloth: acid-free paper)
 ISBN 0-8039-6807-8 (pbk.: acid-free paper)
 1. Class size—United States. I. Title.
 LB3013.2 .A34 1999
 371.2'51—dc21
                                        99-6240

99 00 01 02 03 04 05 10 9 8 7 6 5 4 3 2 1

Production Editor: S. Marlene Head
Editorial Assistant: Kristen L. Gibson
Typesetter: Technical Typesetting, Inc.
Cover Designer: Wendy Hastings Coy

Contents

Preface

The Research Base and Background for This Book

This book builds on the solid foundation of many years of research on class size and student outcomes in the early primary grades of America's public schools. The serious research began in the early 1900s and continues. The Glass and Smith (1978) meta-analysis to show the relation of class size to student achievement, and the Smith and Glass (1979) work to show the relation of class size to classroom practices, teacher satisfaction, and pupil affect started the present round of class-size interest. Their work was followed by studies and books such as Glass, Cahen, Smith, and Filby (1982), Cahen, Filby, McCutcheon, and Kyle (1983), Filby et al. (1980), Indiana's statewide Project Prime Time, and numerous reports and summaries. Except for the meta-analyses, until about 1990, the evidence of a class-size effect was considered inconclusive. Tennessee's large, statewide longitudinal study provided experimental evidence of class-size effects to support the two Glass and Smith meta-analyses.

Although it may be desirable to have small classes throughout education if we expect youngsters to become lifelong learners, this book directly addresses only areas where substantial research can support the claims and suggestions it contains. The ideas and examples expressed here may be transferred to other grades, but the thoughtful reader must make that transfer. The goal of making the recent important research on the "class size effect" clear and useful is its own major challenge.

The knowledge base for this book is the considerable research that has been done on class size and student outcomes. The primary research sources are the studies associated with the Student/Teacher Achievement Ratio (STAR) effort conducted in kindergarten through Grade 3 in Tennessee, beginning in 1984 with the DuPont Study and continuing into 1999 or longer with studies built upon STAR's experimental results. Researchers have followed the progress of STAR students and have used the STAR database to answer important education questions. Major STAR-related studies that constitute the heart of the database include the Lasting Benefits Study (LBS), during which researchers tracked STAR students in Grades 4–9 to check on the magnitude and duration of the initial benefits achieved from being in a small class. Project Challenge was a policy implementation of STAR's small-class findings in 16 relatively poor and low-scoring Tennessee school districts. In the ongoing STAR follow-up studies, researchers are analyzing high school outcomes and social benefits related to a student's class size in Grades K–3. Participation in school was studied in Grades 4 and 8.

STAR Principal Investigators (PIs) and other researchers have used STAR findings to help design and conduct class-size research or demonstration efforts in High Point and in Burke County, North Carolina. Project SAGE in Wisconsin, the Fairfax County, Virginia analyses, and other studies provided added data. Results reported here have been identified and substantiated in meta-analyses and research reviews, in statewide research, in a major experiment, and in other large studies and projects dealing with class size and school improvement.

This book contains vignettes, stories of experiences in small classes, and observations provided by persons who are conducting small classes in primary grades. These practitioner examples demonstrate some good times and bad times in the move from larger to smaller classes. They clarify what can be done and explain differences that occur in smaller rather than in larger classes. Stories, analogies, and examples donated by folks in the front lines can be used as evidence for supporters who advocate small classes in school and for persons who respond to the critics of small classes for small children.

A Couple of Disclaimers

Nothing in this text is meant to say or imply that class size is the long-sought "silver bullet" to solve all education problems. Appropriate continuing professional development should improve a teacher's ability to help youngsters learn. Some youngsters might require one-to-one tutoring (the ultimate class-size reduction), and these intense treatments may still be needed for difficult tasks, even when youngsters begin their schooling in smaller classes. Poorly implemented class-size reductions may not provide the benefits obtained in Project STAR and in the other studies used as data sources for this volume. Other things being equal, however, teachers who have smaller classes will, on average, experience greater student successes over time than will teachers with larger classes.

New knowledge and data require changes in practice. This is to be expected. Experimentation continues. The knowledge base expands, and teachers use and improve upon what is known. Change is the inevitable path to the future. Education can't make everything better (overcome poverty or abuse, rectify home problems, etc.), but without it, there is one less path. The message is that we can do better in education. We can choose to spend education's limited resources better. Why don't we?

A solid foundation for lifelong learning begins in small classes in public elementary schools. This book relates class size to many education issues. The question no longer is, "What should we do to improve education for young children?" The questions are, "Why aren't we doing what the research says?" and "How can we get on with this task?"

Acknowledgments

Many, many people contributed to the long class-size expedition that has led up to this book. The sheer magnitude and duration of the research that preceded this small explanation of parts of it mean that undoubtedly I shall have forgotten to thank someone who made the path easier. For any omissions, I apologize in advance. Fellow so-journers not mentioned individually here are surely referenced in the text. Thanks for the background work, ideas, and support.

Many students, teachers, other educators, and parents made class-size studies possible. Concerned legislators and leaders funded major class-size efforts. The Glass and Smith (1978) meta-analysis rekindled interest in class size and achievement; the Smith and Glass (1979) meta-analysis identified nonacademic benefits of small classes.

Professors and students at four Tennessee Universities were STAR (Student Teacher Achievement Ratio) Principal Investigators (PIs): Fred Bellott and John Johnston (University of Memphis), C. M. Achilles with M. Lintz (University of Tennessee, UT), Helen Pate-Bain with J. B. Zaharias and B. D. Fulton (Tennessee State University, TSU), and John Folger with C. Breda (Vanderbilt University) conducted Project STAR. Jeremy Finn did the primary analyses of STAR and other class-size data. Elizabeth Word directed and monitored STAR for the Tennessee State Department of Education. After STAR's experimental portion, the PIs recommended that the database be housed at TSU in the Center of Excellence for Research in Basic Skills in recognition of Helen Bain's long-standing class-size work. B. A. Nye directed the Center.

A small state grant funded class-size observational research in schools in High Point and Greensboro, North Carolina. Concerned persons began and supported small classes in Burke County, North Carolina, and personnel from SERVE (Southeastern Regional Vision for Education), a federal education laboratory, offered training and evaluation help. In addition to the teachers, students, parents, administrators, and school board members, others directly involved in the North Carolina studies included A. Aust, P. Egelson, S. Gwynn, P. Harman, C. Hicks, W. Honeycutt, K. Kiser-Kling, J. Owen, and T. Stewart. Teachers from Burke County, Rockingham County, Oxford, and High Point, North Carolina contributed stories, vignettes, and views inside their classrooms.

Greta Nagel (California State University, Long Beach) graciously took time from her own responsibilities to add vignettes from California's massive class-size reduction (CSR) effort. Greta enjoys collecting stories, but more importantly, she shares those CSR stories.

Jean Krieger, an elementary school administrator in Louisiana, and Robert Egelson, a child psychologist in North Carolina, contributed insights about small classes. Teachers at Hillcrest Elementary shared their successes along with their teaching and portfolio strategies, and let researchers videotape some small classes. Sheldon Etheridge used federal and state resources to build small learning communities for young children in South Carolina.

Portions of the work reported in the text were supported by the National Education Association, the American Federation of Teachers, funding sources mentioned above, and a grant from the Spencer Foundation entitled A Study of Class Size and At-Risk Students. This book, however, does not necessarily reflect the beliefs or positions of any external funding source.

Thanks to editors of sources in which portions of these data and narratives have been published before, either in the form used here (especially in Chapter 5, What Does it Take to Learn? The Effects of Class Size on Learning), or in slightly different form: *School Business Affairs; Plain Talk About Kids: Transforming Crisis Into Success* (A. P. Thomas, Ed.), Educators Publishing Service, Inc.

Helen Bain carried her passion for helping students and teachers from her presidency of the National Education Association (1970–1971) to legislators and educators in Tennessee, and energized Project STAR. *Special* thanks go to Tennessee legislators and leaders who initiated STAR; to teachers, parents, and students who made STAR live; and to my colleagues who conducted STAR and contributed to this work over so many years. It's a great journey, but much distance remains between here and the goal.

Thanks to anonymous reviewers who helped shape the text and to the professionals at Corwin Press. Robb Clouse, Acquisitions Editor, saw to the details, and Gracia Alkema, President, encouraged me to do "just this one more" book.

Susan Achilles proofed, edited, and suggested: Joanna Warder typed, formatted, retyped, retyped.... Nevertheless, any problems and glitches that remain here are my own. I apologize in advance.

This book is dedicated to adults who put kids first, to teachers and others who do small classes, to policy persons who make small classes possible, and to Helen P. Bain who keeps class-size issues alive.

Thanks to you all.

Charles M. Achilles, Geneva, New York.

About the Author

Charles M. Achilles is a generalist who has researched school issues, including desegregation, effective schools, public confidence, educational cooperatives, preparation of administrators, and class-size effects on pupil achievement and development in primary grades. He has been principal investigator on several nationally recognized studies, such as Project STAR (TN) and Success Starts Small, two major studies of class size and student achievement. He is coauthor of several books, including *Inside Classrooms; Finding Funding: Grantwriting, Fundraising, and Partnerships; Handbook on Gangs in Schools; Let's Make a Deal;* and *Problem Analysis: Responding to School Complexity.* He has published more than 400 items in the professional literature, including reports in Education Resources Information Centers (ERIC).

Currently a Professor of Educational Leadership at Eastern Michigan University, he was Professor and Department Chair at the University of North Carolina at Greensboro. He worked for more than 20 years in educational administration and at the Bureau of Educational Research and Services at the University of Tennessee, Knoxville. He served at the (former) U.S. Office of Education and as a researcher at the University of California, Berkeley, after being a teacher and administrator in public and private schools. As a lecturer for Nova Southeastern University, he meets educators on the "front lines" from whom he learns about problems in the schools.

Achilles holds an A.B. in Classics, an M.A. in Education and Latin, and an Ed.S. and an Ed.D. in Educational Administration, all from the University of Rochester, New York.

Getting
Class Size Right

And then my heart with pleasure fills,
And dances with the daffodils.

William Wordsworth

They are a bunch of flowers growing in a
garbage can.

Ohio teacher in Hayden (1996)

Prologue: Would That It Were More Myth Than Truth

Dateline: *Erehwon. April 1, 1984. The parents of Pat Smith, a first grader, just petitioned the school board for larger classes for the kids.*

A National Education Association (NEA) advertisement titled, "We need a little class" has appeared in several media outlets. If education is to be a class act and if America's schools are to become world class, one place to consider improvement is at the *class* level. This improvement, for once, will directly benefit the young children in schools.

At about 5 years of age, many of America's children bubble over with the joy of going to school. They wait expectantly to ride the big yellow bus or walk to school in small groups. It's a new experience. Until now, the education system's new pupil, Pat, has lived in a small, usually caring community, where s/he was the center of adult attention and played in small groups. Most of what Pat did was unstructured and approvingly accepted with little judgmental pressure by playmates and adults alike.

In all too many situations, that childhood idyll ends abruptly when Pat enters the school to begin a mandatory sentence of compulsory education. Hey, Pat, here are 25–35 new workmates. Here is a new adult called teacher who will share one adult's attention with the entire class. This adult will grade whatever you do and decide if you're a sparrow or a red bird. Gone, Pat, are the familiar folks. In their place are strangers. Hello there, big world.

> Ah, happy hills, ah pleasing shade,
> Ah fields beloved in vain,
> Where once my careless childhood strayed,
> a stranger yet to pain.
>
> Sir Thomas Gray,
> "An Ode on a Distant Prospect of Eton College"

The class that Pat joins is big, and the school that houses the class is even bigger. Some elementary schools house 1000 or more strangers, many children and some adults with funny "names": secretary, nurse, principal, media specialist, teacher aide, cafeteria worker, volunteer, plant engineer. Wow. Except for the new kids on the block, the children at this school are mostly older than Pat. They already have experience in a world called school. Some speak different languages and are of a different race or sex or background than Pat. These new people present challenges for Pat, and so does this huge new building, surrounded by asphalt, cars, buses, fences, and some playgrounds. Schools can be good news or bad news. They have new sounds, smells, sights—daunting.

If the shock of moving from a small, intimate play group into a veritable mob scene isn't enough, many Pats will enter dilapidated, dark, dreary, dungeon-like schools. The General Accounting Office (GAO) estimates a $120–200 billion unfunded liability just to bring America's schools up to safety and building codes. By adult mandates, laws, or policy these very young children will be placed into work groups much larger than those in which adults work, often in crumbling and crowded work spaces that few adults would voluntarily inhabit. As if the dramatic changes in social and physical arrangements were not traumatic enough, Pat and other little colleagues have encountered one of the schools described by Kozol (1970) in *Savage Inequalities,* and one documented by Hayden (1996) in the Corporation for Public Broadcasting film *Children in America's Schools.* This documentary, narrated by Bill Moyers, portrays in stark comparison some run-down schools and some new, well-equipped learning centers and campuses. Is this dismal beginning of "education" what America's youngest school children deserve? Is it what adults want for children? Are these conditions expected to start a child on a long and important journey to literacy, numeracy, and citizenship?

He scans the ceiling, nearly three stories over his head, light fixtures like star bursts. "Whoa. What a place," he says. To Danny, whose generation has lived out their school life in portable classrooms, that taxpayers would foot the bills for a structure on this scale is, I suppose, a novelty. [A discussion of a correctional facility]

Martini (1994, p. 154)

If they could divine the future, some of these young children might stand tall and shout the Roman gladiator's classic greeting, *Morituri te salutamus* (we who are about to die salute you). Already bending under the weight of shackles such as poverty and abuse, some Pats shuffle along to school where they will get only a little more attention in their class of 30 or so than they will as latch-key kids later in the day.

Other Pats, however, are more fortunate in one respect. Their schoolhouse doors open upon a modern, air-conditioned, and carpeted facility with central air (instead of screenless windows) and heat (instead of a coal-fired furnace). The outer trappings of these schools are okay, pleasing, comfortable; however, the other half of the scenario, the number of young children herded into a room with strangers, is the same. Lots of new people. Lots and lots of them. Different. Some Pats will succeed anyway.

Some Pats are exceptionally lucky. They go to work in fine facilities with only 15 or so other young people in ample-sized space. A few will go to exclusive private schools with good facilities and only 8–15 other age-mates working with one teacher. They will succeed for sure. After all, success is the hallmark of private schools.

> Now we must make our public elementary and secondary schools the best in the world . . . and every parent already knows the key, good teachers and small classes. Tonight I propose the first-ever national effort to reduce class size in the early grades. . . . With these teachers, we will reduce class size in the first, second, and third grades to an average of 18 students in a class.
>
> Clinton (1998)

As Social Problems Intensify, Class Size
Steps to the Forefront Once More

Signs are emerging on two fronts that some politicians may finally be putting kids first: (a) President Clinton recommended adding teachers to reduce class sizes in early elementary grades and (b) actions in states throughout the nation are moving class sizes in elementary classrooms to manageable levels.

Importantly, class-size policy initiatives and legislation reflect the happy marriage of solid research and common sense, something that often is all too uncommon. Class-size changes seem to be driven, at least partly, by lingering perceptions that American education somehow is "failing," and that kids today neither know as much nor behave as well as today's adults did in their former golden years.

The education debate begun by President Clinton's 1998 recommendation to add enough classroom teachers so that elementary class sizes can eventually be reduced to a level where teachers can work effectively and students can learn productively may be in time to help save the next generation of children. Appropriately sized groups for the important foundation of learning to learn are the starting point for each person's education future. This new foundation, currently discussed at about 15 students to 1 teacher (15:1), or perhaps 18:1, needs to happen when the child first enters the formal education environment. Small classes are preventive, not remedial. What factors are driving people's attention to class size? One event is the accumulating research information on the benefits of small classes.

[STAR] ... is the most significant educational research done in the US during the past 25 years.

Orlich (1992, p. 632)

A Synopsis of Project STAR

The Student Teacher Achievement Ratio (STAR) effort was a true education experiment with more than 11,600 youngsters and 1000 teachers assigned at random during STAR's four years (1985–1989). Some students were assigned to classes of approximately 15 youngsters and 1 teacher (15:1) designated as small (S) classes. Others were assigned to classes averaging about 25 youngsters and 1 teacher (25:1) designated as the regular (R) classes or the control group. Regular classes of about 25 youngsters with a teacher and a full-time teacher aide (RA) were a second experimental condition in Project STAR. To maintain the rigor of an experiment, students were assigned to one of the three conditions when they first entered public school, usually in Kindergarten (K), but sometimes in Grade 1. Teachers were assigned at random to class conditions each year.

Researchers have used STAR's large database to explore many education questions related to class size to understand more about the positive results of early class-size research and to learn how class-size results can be used to improve education. For example, researchers examined such issues as random vs. nonrandom assignment of students in Grades K–3 by using STAR's randomly established regular-sized classes and the nonrandomly assigned students in 21 comparison schools located in STAR school districts. (Added details of STAR's design, including an explanation of the comparison schools are in later chapters.) The STAR researchers have considered school size and class size, class-size effects to reduce the achievement gap between minority and nonminority students, student behavior and discipline, the impact of class size on student participation and engagement in schooling and identification with schools, and other class-size issues.

Some STAR-related class-size studies were student dissertations or separate inquiries of STAR principal investigators (PIs) to satisfy questions that arose during STAR or to check questions posed by external reviewers of STAR. Some studies were to clarify and extend ideas raised during STAR, such as the confusion surrounding the concepts of class size and pupil teacher ratio (PTR), and the full-term (K–12) benefits of starting school in a small class. Topics of some STAR-related class-size studies and the authors or PIs of the studies appear in summary form in Table 1.1. Each abbreviated title in Table 1.1 identifies the general question of interest or the focus of the inquiry.

Table 1.1 demonstrates the magnitude and breadth of the STAR-related class-size information base from which many generalizations and examples in this text have been drawn. Results of studies listed in Table 1.1 plus earlier class-size studies and meta-analyses of class-size studies such as the work of Glass and Smith (1978) are used to substantiate positions and comments made throughout the text. A review of STAR prompted Harvard University Professor Emeritus Frederick Mosteller (1995) to comment:

> ... the Tennessee class size project ... is one of the most important investigations ever carried out ... in the field of education. (p. 113)

TABLE 1.1 Samples of the STAR Legacy, Class-Size Studies, Categorized as "Subsidiary" (directly from STAR), "Ancillary" (building on the STAR database), and "Related" (usually involving STAR researchers)

Category, Title, & Purpose[a]	Date(s)	Author(s), Source, Publication Date
STAR (Class-size experiment)	1985–1989	Word et al., 1990 Finn & Achilles, 1990
Subsidiary Studies		
• Lasting benefits study	1989–1996	Nye, Achilles, Boyd-Zaharias, Fulton, & Wallenhorst, 1994
• Project Challenge (TN)	1989–1996	Nye, Achilles, Boyd-Zaharias, Fulton, & Wallenhorst, 1994
• Participation, Grades 4, 8	1990, 1996	Finn, 1989, 1993; Voelkl, 1995; Finn, Fulton, Zaharias, & Nye, 1989 Finn & Cox, 1992
• STAR Follow-Up Studies	1996–1999	HEROS, 1997
Ancillary Studies (use or extend STAR)		
• Retention in grade	1994–1995	Harvey, 1994, 1995
• Achievement gap	1993–1995	Bingham, 1993, 1994
• Value of K in classes of varying sizes (test scores)	1985–1989	Achilles, Nye, & Bain, 1994-95
• School size and class-size issues	1985–1989	Nye, 1995
• Random v. nonrandom pupil assignment and achievement	1985–1989	Zaharias et al., 1995
• Class size and discipline Grades 3, 5, 7	1989, 1991, 1996	Several studies. SSS, 1995; Hibbs, 1997.
• Outstanding teacher analysis (top 10% of STAR teachers)	1985–1989	Bain et al., 1992
• Teacher aides		Zaharias & Bain, 1998; Achilles et al., 1993
Related Studies		
• Success Starts Small: Grade 1 in 1:14 and 1:23 schools	1993–1995	Achilles et al., 1994 Kiser-Kling, 1995

(continued)

TABLE 1.1 Continued

Category, Title, & Purpose[a]	Date(s)	Author(s), Source, Publication Date
• Burke Co., NC study	1992–1999	Achilles et al., 1994 SERVE
• Education production functions	1996–1999	Krueger, 1997, 1998

[a] This is a sample of STAR-related class-size studies. Not all authors appear exactly as listed here. A similar table appears in several STAR reports.

Declining Conditions of Children and Schools Require Class-Size Action Now

The time is long past when American adults should have considered education and the future seriously. As with bank accounts or the education savings accounts that appease wealthy parents, the enlightened future requires investment—an investment in America's children. Until the age of required schooling, the investment in children is primarily the responsibility of the social institution called family. The changing conditions of the American family are not the topic here, but these documented changes do have important bearings upon the nature of almost all other American social institutions: religion, government, health and welfare, business and economics, protection (military and police), and especially upon education.

The concern here, however, is about education. Educators should be advocates for young children and should encourage all adults, especially adults in policy roles, to invest in children through careful use of research. Calls for changing how we treat and educate children come from many sources. The data that describe the current generation of children are unpleasant. Concerns for America's children have been advanced by demographers such as Hodgkinson (1991, 1992, 1996), who pinpointed the growth of child poverty, diversity, and related education problems; by pediatricians such as Hamburg (1992), who explained the obstacles that young children face in American society; by educational researchers such as Cooley (1993), who described the "difficulty of the educational task" and emphasized the intersections of costs, schooling, family, poverty, and education; by educators and academics such as Steinberg, Brown and Dornbusch (1996), who studied education change and explained that parents must help in the education effort—that parents and the community must get involved and accept their share of responsibility for improving the conditions for schooling.

Using data in Pennsylvania, Cooley (1993) calculated that over 60% of the "variation in average school performance (test scores) among these school districts can be explained by these three simple census factors" of a child:

1) living in poverty
2) with a single parent,
3) who is not a high-school graduate. (p. 5)

It is overwhelmingly tough for single, poor, working parents to be active in schools and to assure constant supervision for their children. Yet, parent or family-involvement research and school-improvement reports describe a parent's efforts as important in helping students succeed in schools. Steinberg et al. (1996) explained that parents need to take an active role in education. Education is a cooperative effort.

The need for educators to emphasize the early years of schooling is clearly evident in the demographic data for America provided by Hodgkinson (1992) and other demographers. Check just a few dreary scenes.

1. In 1990, 13%, of all children were regularly hungry; 25% were born to unmarried parents; over 20% of all children under age 18 were poor; about 350,000 were born to drug-addicted mothers, 19% had no health insurance, and 166 of every 100,000 juveniles were incarcerated. (Hodgkinson, 1992, p. 4)

2. The fastest growing group in the US was prisoners . . . we now have a higher percentage of our population behind bars than does any other nation . . . 82% of our prisoners are dropouts. (Hodgkinson, 1992, p. 3)

3. The "Norman Rockwell" family—a working father, a housewife mother, and two children of public school age—constituted only 6% of U.S. households for most of the decade (of the 1980s). (Hodgkinson, 1992, p. 3)

4. Every day in America 40 teen-age girls give birth to their third child. To be the third child of a child is to be

> very much at risk ... teen-ager mothers tend to give birth to premature children ... prematurity leads to low birth weight, which is a good predictor of major learning difficulties. Thus, about 700,000 of the annual cohort of 3.3 million babies (21%) are almost assured of being either educationally retarded or difficult to teach. (Hodgkinson, 1992, pp. 4–5)

Annual reports from the Annie E. Casey Foundation track the condition of children in the United States, and by states and urban areas. The *Kids Count* data books describe children who need serious consideration. Hodgkinson's (1992) scenes of poverty suffered by America's youngest children and the trends apparent in the *Kids Count* data books might make Dickens blanch. The growth of U.S. child poverty was updated by a Census Bureau study. The following snippets were taken from an interview with the acting director of the Institute for Research on Poverty at the University of Wisconsin.

> **Question: Who's in trouble now?** Clearly the children. In recent years, we had 15 million poor children and the poverty rate has been over 20%. This rate is embarrassingly high relative to other industrial countries. In Sweden and Denmark, it's less than 5%. Germany, around 7%. Great Britain and Canada, 10% to 12%.
>
> **Question: Why such a jump in the child poverty rate?** There's been a demographic earthquake. The number of children living in vulnerable situations has increased dramatically.
>
> **Question: How do other countries keep the rate down?** They simply invest a lot more in children. They have much more widely available child care. They have more universal programs than in this country. *For roughly $11 of the federal budget that we spend on the elderly, we spend $1 on kids.* We're very child and family unfriendly [emphasis added]. (*USA Today,* 9/26/96, p. 6A; used with permission)

"There's been a demographic earthquake."

(*USA Today,* 1996)

The video, *Children in America's Schools* (Hayden, 1996) portrayed the shameful warehousing of children in decrepit facilities that caused one Ohio teacher to say of the little students, "They are a bunch of flowers growing in a garbage can." This callous indifference toward children—or even worse, squalor consciously imposed on children—is taking a gruesome toll that is indirectly evident in the education-bashing stories that media seem to thrive on: gangs, the dramatic increases in students needing special services, drugs, violence, low test scores, and even graduates who are not literate. How to ameliorate these conditions is the task of professional educators working with parents and other caring adults. Surely, beginning the education experience of our very youngest children more humanely and more effectively than is the norm today will sow a rich harvest of returns.

[America] ... very child and family unfriendly.

(*USA Today*, 1996)

Poverty and discontinuities in the typical "Norman Rockwell" American family that education was originally developed to serve add heavy weight to the already numbing burden that educators tackle in classrooms. Pressures on educators to meet standards are increased when children become the pawns of special interests, when education is the bargain basement for tax-abatement-seeking corporations, and schools are laboratories for each fad that comes along promising to save education. Consider the added pressures to solving the challenges strewn in the path of long-term education when successful early intervention programs such as Head Start are available to only a few of the eligible students because of the increasing numbers of poverty-level children (Hodgkinson, 1985, pp. 8-9).

Young Children as the Future View

American education has historically served a "melting pot" function, bringing hope to generations of foreign-born citizens and to persons of modest means who look to formal schooling for language, enculturation, and economic advancement. The challenges of educating children are magnified when the children speak languages other than English or come from cultures different from the "mainstream" inhabited by many teachers. As America becomes more and more diverse, the diversity is far more evident in the younger generation than among the citizens who typically control policy and politics in America. Analyses of governing boards, legislatures, and even school boards show that people in those groups are disproportionately more white, middle class, male, and second (or more) generation American than are the children for whom the boards are making the rules, policies, and laws. Unless policy persons have a future orientation, generational differences evolve into an unrealistic "good old days" view that does not serve children well. To get a first-hand view of generational differences near you and to peek at the near future, try the exercise, "One Future View," presented in Figure 1.1.

ONE FUTURE VIEW

If you want to know what society will be like in the near future, don't look at older people, or at people currently making policy for young children. Look at the children. They are the future. One way to bring the future into present focus is to study today's children who are the demographic harbingers of tomorrow. Try this exercise with data from your community, from a large city, from your state, or from the United States.

Examine demographic data for people ± 3 years from your own age. Examine the same data for the same geographic area for children, for example, ages 1–5, or for a demographic division you can easily obtain. You are looking at tomorrow and comparing it with today. How does it look? What responsibility do educators have for molding the "tomorrows?"

Figure 1.1. Exercise to Estimate a Future Bilt From Today's Data

Educators Must Put Kids First

Learning and education are lifelong experiences. Although people learn on their own throughout their lives, a society supports the institution of education to formalize the transmission of important knowledge and the preparation of youngsters for later life. Education complements and extends learning experiences provided by other groups and institutions such as the economic sector or religion. Everyone benefits when the young of a society grow up to perpetuate and advance that society.

Formal education starts early in life, perhaps with some pre-kindergarten (pre-K) experiences such as Head Start, but more commonly the education journey starts with K followed by 12 years in a graded school. Teachers are advocates for young pupils who don't yet have the skills to make key education choices for themselves. Building desired decision-making skills and initiating life-long learning are important purposes of education.

☺ A former sixth—grade teacher in southern California was reassigned to a second-grade class as part of the class-size reduction program at her school. Going from a class of 34 large, upper-grade bodies to one with only 20 small bodies meant that she was physically more involved with the students at writing times. Not only was she able to move among the desks freely, even taking a small chair with her from student to student, but she had time to chat with most students about their writing during a typical writing period. Writing times became coaching times, and long hours of marking papers at home gave way to interacting with students about their writing right there on the spot in the classroom.

Using small classes for little children is not a new idea. What is new is that small-class education is now well researched. Using small groups meets the dual tests of common sense and of widespread use elsewhere, not only in education. Small classes, or their equivalent, are already accepted and commonly employed by adults in their workplaces and in social groups. Yet, small classes may meet adult resistance when they are considered for very young children. This is, indeed, one strange conundrum that educators face.

Using small classes for little children is not a new idea. What
is new is that small-class education is now well researched and
the research supports common sense.

Class Size: What It Is, and What It Isn't

Throughout this book, the term *class size* refers to *the number of youngsters who regularly appear in a teacher's classroom and for whom that
teacher is primarily responsible and accountable.* These are the youngsters you would count if you observed a teacher's classroom day in
and day out, the youngsters on the teacher's class roster.

Except in rare cases, class size is not the same as the pupil–
teacher ratio (PTR). The PTR is a derived estimate commonly computed by dividing the number of youngsters at a site, such as at a
building, by the number of professionals who work at or serve that
site. The professionals might include special teachers, administrators, coordinators, counselors, media persons, and so forth. Sometimes a student-to-adult ratio is used as the PTR, and that may include noncertified but important support staff, such as teacher aides,
custodians, food-service and transportation personnel, and maybe
even volunteers to make the site's PTR attractive (say 10:1). A *small
PTR* is a badge of honor among schools and a point that they advertise to attract more students. Expensive private schools advertise
small classes.

This book is about class size, not about PTR. This is not a semantic game or a trivial distinction. The difference in the United States
between PTR and class size is often more than 10 students per
classroom, and this difference speaks much about the fragmented,
project-driven nature of a child's education experience in American
schools.

Class Size and PTR Are Birds of a Different Feather

Doesn't everybody know the difference between class size and PTR?
Maybe they don't, or they haven't really thought about it. Critics
of small class size may not understand the difference between PTR
and class size. Maybe they just substitute one term for the other as

synonyms. Although the distinction between class size and PTR is extremely important as a base for education policy and in planning, conducting, and assessing education, this distinction is consistently blurred in discussions and criticisms of education.

Class-size critics may not understand the difference between PTR and class size.

Two examples highlight the confusion that imprecise use of terms can cause. In the examples provided here, the authors cited write about education and probably know the differences between PTR and class size. If when they say "class size" the authors mean "PTR," their conclusions may be correct. If they really mean class size, the weight of evidence supports smaller classes. In each quote, PTR and class size appear as synonyms in the same sentence.

> Since 87% of them (teachers) are public employees, it follows that policy-makers' decisions have great impact. A policy decision to employ more teachers (such as by reducing *pupil-teacher ratios,* which have fallen from 27 to 1 to 17 to 1 over the past 40 years) is obviously different from a decision to hold *class size* constant but pay teachers more— or invest more in technology ... *recognizing that ever-smaller classes are a costly and ineffectual recipe* for improved student performance.
>
> (C. Finn, 1997, pp. 48, 36; emphasis added)

> Most discussions of reducing class size begin with an assertion that student performance will increase if only *class sizes* can be reduced, a proposition shown to be generally erroneous. They then move quickly to policies *of large-scale reductions* in *pupil-teacher ratios* where there is no direct linkage *between specific class size decisions and student performance.* The situation and the educational outcomes might change dramatically if everybody had stronger incentives to use budgets wisely and to improve student performance.
>
> (Hanushek, 1998, p. 36; emphasis added)

Class size influences student outcome positively (e.g., Finn & Achilles, 1990; Robinson, 1990; Wenglinsky, 1997) and PTR doesn't influence outcomes very much as shown in studies (e.g., Boozer & Rouse, 1995) and in evaluations of Title I, a PTR-driven and teacher-aide laden program (e.g., Abt Associates, 1997; Borman & D'Agostino, 1996; Wong & Meyer, 1998). Project STAR provided experimental evidence that full-time teacher aides in the classroom do not influence outcomes much (Boyd-Zaharias & Pate-Bain, 1998; Word et al., 1990). As explained later, differences between class size and PTR offer choices that could make small classes more widespread, less expensive, less hectic to implement, and perhaps far more effective and efficient than the larger classes that are now used.

The terms *class size* and *PTR* are frequently misused . . .

Why Are There Critics of Small Classes?

Some individuals and groups continue to argue that something might be more appropriate for improving education than to start students in small classes when they begin their sojourn of 13 or more years through the public education system. Critics seldom explain what that something is, or the research base for it, or how to do it (for example, hire better teachers). Differing positions and points of view deserve to be made public. In this way, ideas can be part of an open debate so that important research-driven and data-based changes can be made. Positive criticism and healthy, informed skepticism of constructive critics can improve the entire process. In the case of schooling for young children, however, alternative policies and ideas should be built upon research evidence about education benefits for young children and upon the experiences of successful teachers and parents. Importantly, the ideas to improve public schooling should also strengthen the cornerstones of American democracy. The ideals of public education are built upon Jefferson's admonition that a nation that "wishes to be ignorant and free, wishes what never was and never will be," and upon social values such as quality, equality, and equity.

Widespread use of small classes for early grades can dramatically change the landscape of public education. Pet projects, ideas of special-interest groups, and traditions will be challenged. Change brings concurrent shifts in power relationships and in distribution of resources. Persons who believe that they may lose something in shifts of power and resources can be expected to take strong stands against the change. People who are uncertain about how change will influence their known, comfortable, routine activities may resist change. No wonder that changes elicit strong feelings.

For example, small classes in elementary grades should disrupt the current practice of using a myriad of special projects to address each perceived problem facing the schools. The project-driven mentality to "fix" schools is highlighted by the crazy quilt of categorical funding for education. This project-mentality approach to try to stem the rising torrent of challenges for educators presents a great metaphor for people old enough to remember tires with inner tubes. Conjure up the image of education as an inner tube trying to inflate the wheels of progress. Unfortunately, the tires' old black-rubber inner tubes have become splotched all over, measles-like, with small red-rubber patches, each disconnected one from the other, and each a prime candidate for a blow out. Education needs tubeless new tires. Even education's critics will profit from the better ride in the long run.

Public education touches everyone. Education must not be an unfunded mandate and a public liability that occurs when policy-makers require expensive changes without providing the funds to support those changes. Education becomes an unfunded liability when the public does not provide resources so the schools that students are required to attend will at least meet local building or fire codes. Educators face an unfunded mandate when higher standards are imposed without support to improve working conditions so that they and their students can achieve the new standards. One other example of limiting conditions imposed upon students is a steady upward creep in class sizes in early grades.

Public education touches everyone.

Classes of about 15 to 18 students and one teacher (15:1 or so) may need an initial investment that will return solid economic and social benefits in later years, if research is correct. In setting the policy requiring school attendance and in contemplating funding levels, adults may wish to recall poet Robert Service's line in *The Cremation of Sam McGee*: "Now a promise made is a debt unpaid, and the trail has its own stern code." Do policies about schooling constitute "a promise made?" If the debt remains unpaid, do poor conditions in schooling build a trail that has a stern code? Does that code of the trail spell out violence, gangs, low scores, lack of participation in democratic processes?

"A promise made is a debt unpaid."

Robert Service

Small Classes: A Direct Pipeline to the Students

Establishing appropriately sized classes in early primary grades benefits the children in the classrooms first, foremost, and directly. There is no need for any middleman, peddler, or vendor to skim part of the funds. Secondary beneficiaries are the teachers and families of young children in those classes. The contingent beneficiaries of putting kids first will be society as a whole. In this sense, establishing appropriately sized classes for young children represents an investment in the future. That's what conscientious educators are about. "A promise made. . . ."

What are the trade-offs and choices involved in making the promise of a good education to young children? Whenever there are competing ideologies, limited funds, and options, people make choices. Public-sector choices are played out in the arenas of policy and politics. Elected officials set policies to direct public choices. Policies can be more rational when they are based upon careful research and available data than if they are enacted without supporting data. There may also be several paths to the same goal. For example, to lose weight, I can reduce caloric intake, or keep caloric intake about the same and increase an exercise program to burn off more calories. A third choice is to combine the first two options. At this time, there is no claim that smaller rather than larger classes is the only trail to improve education. Undeniably, however, small classes are part of the "promise made."

The young of America enter the schoolhouse door at ages 4, 5, or 6. That door can open on a stairway to hope or a dungeon of despair. ("All hope abandon, ye who enter here.") Some children enter vile facilities heated by coal, with leaking roofs, inadequate space and electric connections, and defective plumbing. Increasingly more children enter school today than in past years dramatically unprepared for the demands of schooling. Instead of being inducted, apprenticed, or mentored, like many adults entering new careers, young kids new to school are mixed with 25–35 strangers in an entirely foreign setting. They are expected not only to learn the norms of this new workplace, but also to know how to go to the bathroom without assistance, handle cafeteria lines and buses, be brave and not cry, and to have perfect attendance and manners. Oh, yes, they also should like the place so well that they will stay in education 12, 14, 16, or more years and love learning well enough to become lifelong learners, contributors to a strong economy and to a great experiment in democracy, and be constructive participants in government and society without succumbing to drugs, gangs, or other illegal acts. In a mob scene. At age 5. Alone. Amazing.

Jean is a new teacher. Having completed 13 public-school years, K–12, and 4 college years, Jean begins work in Pat's school. Although successful in at least 17 years of schooling, Jean receives new-teacher orientation and materials, in-service help both for new skills and as an introduction to the "way we do things around here." Special new-teacher induction programs and periodic on-the-job training sessions for first-year teachers make Jean feel welcome and are designed to assure Jean's success. The district's award-winning mentor-teacher program provides Jean with a caring, experienced master teacher to answer questions, give advice, and keep the road to success straight and pothole-free. Compare Jean's kid-glove treatment *after* 17 or more years of education success with Pat's sink-or-swim, boot-camp introduction to what society hopes will be a 17-year road *to* success.

Still More Questions Than Answers

Although material in this book will provide some answers, more than that, the material should clarify issues and raise new questions.

An intriguing challenge is not to answer a question, but to raise new questions that start people thinking and behaving differently about education. Catch a little bit of question-asking enthusiasm.

Ask important questions. Use research to form reasoned answers to important questions.

2

Recent Antecedents
of Class-Size Interest

... there's a reason to life! We can lift ourselves out of ignorance, we can find ourselves as creatures of excellence and
intelligence and skill.

(Bach, *Jonathan Livingston Seagull*, pp. 30–31)

The question of a class-size effect in education is hardly new. Peri-
odically, class size emerges as a topic of considerable interest and
debate. Parents and teachers like small classes, and the idea squares
with common sense. What is the background of the current class-size
interest?

Some Critics Are Correct: Class Size *Is* Old Hat

Plato, Socrates, Aristotle, and other great teachers of antiquity lav-
ished individual attention on their students. They used dialogue,
the Socratic method, and walks and talks in the groves of academe
characteristic of peripateticism. Christian theology includes a Great

Teacher working directly and primarily with a class of 12, but also with larger groups. ("And He opened His mouth and taught them," St. Matthew, chap. 5.) According to Angrist and Lavy (1996), class size and student achievement interest in Jewish education began in the 12th century when Maimonides, the Rabbinic scholar, laid out the principles of class size according to concepts presented in the *Talmud*. Maybe by relying upon the collective wisdom of the ancients we can find ourselves as "creatures of excellence and intelligence and skill."

Some pioneering class-size studies may have been too brief, or conducted in upper grades, or were weakened by unsophisticated design or analyses so that their results were inconclusive or inconsistent. Maybe early studies described as class size were really studies of pupil–teacher ratio (PTR). Large-scale, random-assignment experiments are not common in education. Without random assignment, policies and practices such as assigning low-performing students to small classes can blunt the finding of a class-size effect (Akerhielm, 1995). Several early class-size studies, however, were substantial, and their results consistently favored the small classes. Lindbloom (1970) summarized the reported relationships between class sizes and educational outcomes using results from numerous studies and concluded that the evidence favored small classes and supported the assertion that teachers in small classes use more desirable practices than do teachers in larger classes.

Olson (1971) conducted extensive studies on class size to answer the question, "What effects do class sizes of 5, 15, 25, or 35 have on students?" Olson's odyssey included observations in thousands of elementary and secondary classrooms in about 112 mostly suburban United States schools. Olson rated 51 student and teacher behaviors as positive or negative and related those observations to test scores. Olson found considerable performance-score changes at the 5-, 15-, and 25-student-per-class levels in elementary grades and at the 10- and 15-student levels in secondary schools. Based upon those results and the findings of over 60 other studies, Olson prepared a list of nine defensible generalizations to support the contention that learning conditions and outcomes are improved in small classes. Summaries of Lindbloom's (1970) and Olson's (1971) observations are presented in a later chapter.

The present emphasis on class size probably dates from the Glass and Smith (1978) landmark meta-analysis of class-size studies and their student academic outcomes, and from the Smith and Glass (1979) meta-analysis of class size and teacher, student, and classroom variables. The Glass and Smith work was followed by two publications from the Education Research Service (ERS, 1978, 1980), the publication of an *Experimental Study of the Effects of Class Size* (Shapson, Wright, Eason, & Fitzgerald, 1980), and by results of observations in second grades in two schools (Filby et al., 1980). The Filby et al. study showed that simply reducing class sizes triggered important changes in classroom management, in curriculum presented, and in amount of curriculum covered, among other things.

Except for two books on class size (Cahen, Filby, McCutcheon, & Kyle, 1983; Glass, Cahen, Smith, & Filby, 1982), this foment for future education progress, like many other changes in education direction, was essentially built by looking backward. The renewed interest in class size both in the late 1970s and in the early 1990s was driven by analyses of studies, by observation, and by a growing uneasiness that current, generally poorly researched or evaluated education practices were not addressing the growing problems that society expected education to solve. It seems that the more educated the general population becomes, the more those educated people expect from education, and the more rational and appealing is the idea that small classes provide positive benefits.

While the late 1970s regeneration of class-size interest was being fanned with the publication of a few studies, the state of Indiana launched Project Prime Time (Chase, Mueller, & Walden, 1986). District leaders could lower class sizes to 18:1, or employ a teacher and an instructional aide when class size reached about 24 students. Prime Time had provisions for evaluation, but it was primarily a demonstration project, and not research. It began with the reduction of class sizes in Grades 1 and 2 in participating districts. A local district could reduce class sizes in either kindergarten (K) or Grade 3 in the third year.

Results in Prime Time generally favored small classes, but findings on student achievement were mixed (Chase, Mueller, & Walden, 1986; Mueller, Chase, & Walden, 1988). Prime Time was unevenly implemented, and it included the use of instructional aides as a way to reduce class sizes: Classes with a teacher and an aide were considered small classes. When the results of Tennessee's Project STAR later showed that the use of teacher aides did not generally improve student outcomes, some of Prime Time's lack of consistent results became at least hypothetically clear (Boyd-Zaharias & Pate-Bain, 1998; Word et al., 1990). The use of teacher aides would be a PTR event, not a real class-size adjustment as described in STAR.

Also in the fall of 1984, Helen Bain initiated the DuPont study, a small study in two elementary schools in metro-Nashville, TN. Bain had served as president (1970–1971) of the National Education Association (NEA), where one interest was to get class sizes to a level so teachers could teach and children could learn. The DuPont study showed that students in smaller classes performed better than did students in larger classes (Bain, Achilles, Dennis, Parks, & Hooper, 1988; Whittington, Bain, & Achilles, 1985). However, as in some analyses of Prime Time (e.g., Tillitski, Gilman, Mohr, & Stone, 1988) and Head Start and other early childhood programs (Barnett, 1985, 1995), achievement gains made in the first years seemed to fade by Grade 3. Although the DuPont study was small in size, its impact was large.

DuPont results added positive ammunition to the generally favorable results from Prime Time and from earlier studies such as those by Lindbloom (1970), Olson (1971), and Glass and Smith (1978), and launched a major education inquiry. The Tennessee legislature established a statewide experiment to determine the effects of small classes (about 15 students and one teacher, or 15:1) on the achievement and development of youngsters in Grades K–3. As a hedge against possible large costs of small classes, the legislature also asked researchers to study the relative benefits of a full-time instructional aide with the teacher in a class of about 22–25 pupils. That class-size study, STAR, was part of the negotiations for (then) Governor Lamar Alexander's "Better Schools Program," which received its greatest recognition for a career ladder or incentive-pay component for teachers.

Project STAR and Its Development: Well-Kept Secrets?

Project STAR was a longitudinal, statewide, randomized *experiment*. By 1998, about 11,600 students had been tracked on STAR's database if they had been assigned at random to one of STAR's three conditions. Those three conditions were a small class (S) of approximately 15 students (a range of 13–17) with one teacher (15:1), a regular class (R) averaging 25 students (range of 22–25) or 25:1, and a reg-

TABLE 2.1 Summary of the Experimental (S, RA) and Control (R) Conditions, STAR, 1985–1989

Class Condition	Experimental Range	Mean Size
Small (S)	13–17	15
Regular (R)	22–25	25
Regular with aide (RA)	22–25 (aide)	25

ular class with a full-time instructional aide (RA). STAR originally included 79 schools in 46 of Tennessee's (then) 140 school districts. Each school with one or more S classes, also included at least one of both other conditions (R, RA). The in-school design controlled for building and district variables, addressed the potential Hawthorne effect, obviated control-group mortality, and was parsimonious. Table 2.1 includes a summary of STAR's conditions.

Researchers identified comparison schools ($n = 21$) in STAR districts that matched closely with the STAR schools on key variables. They collected achievement-test data from these comparison schools each year when STAR students were tested. Because the in-school design was rigorous and parsimonious, little use has yet been made of the comparison-school data, except to study the test-score differences in random and nonrandom assignments of pupils in regular-sized classes in STAR and in comparison schools. (Zaharias, 1993; Zaharias, Achilles, & Cain, 1995; Zaharias, Achilles, Nye, & Cain, 1995).

District leaders agreed to participate in STAR for four years. STAR researchers followed youngsters who entered kindergarten in 1985 ($n = 6325$) until they left Grade 3 in 1989. Students were assigned at random to class sizes (S, R, RA) and teachers were assigned at random to classes. About 1500 students who did not enter school in K in 1985 were assigned at random in Grade 1 when they entered STAR schools in 1986. Students essentially remained together each year (cohort). New teachers were assigned as the cohorts moved through the grades. New students to STAR schools were assigned to class types at random. Except for random assignments, the establishment of the S, R, and RA class conditions, and some reassignment of pupils between R and RA classes in first grade when no differences were found between student outcomes in these two groups at the end of kindergarten, researchers changed nothing else in the schools.

The four STAR principal investigators (PIs) represented four Tennessee universities. Advisory boards and panels of experts provided guidance. The project director was from the State Department of Education. To maintain objectivity, an external research design consultant conducted the primary STAR analyses. The PIs also analyzed data and conducted related studies. Several STAR staff members who began with the study were still associated with STAR work in 1999, thus maintaining important continuity and history.

STAR's Progeny

STAR cost over $12 million in its first four years and generated many other studies, some of which have been longitudinal. Researchers in the Lasting Benefits Study (LBS) tracked STAR youngsters to see just how long and to what degree the small-class benefits obtained during STAR would remain. Researchers have conducted the STAR Follow-up Studies to determine the long-term (K–12) outcomes of early STAR benefits, such as courses taken and grades in high school, retention, dropout, and student behavior in and out of school. Project Challenge, which began in 1989–1990, was a policy application of STAR findings. Sixteen of Tennessee's poorest and educationally low-scoring school districts were "challenged" to use the STAR findings to improve their student outcomes. The state provided extra funds to help those districts reduce class sizes. Although Challenge was not an experiment, researchers estimated its results by tracking the average rankings of the Challenge districts among the state rankings of districts on student outcomes in reading and math for Grades 2–4. Following the STAR prototype, the Challenge districts moved up in the state's ranking from their well below average status to near or above average on state tests after three years.

A student's participation in school is important for school success and for remaining in school (Finn, 1989, 1993, 1998). Early school participation carries over into early adult participation in society (Lindsay, 1982, 1984). Using the STAR database, researchers studied the participation in school of youngsters in S, R, and RA at various grades (e.g., Finn & Cox, 1992). Students in S classes had quantitatively more and qualitatively more positive participation than did students in R and RA classes. Many other STAR-related studies have been conducted. Some of those studies are shown in Table 1.1.

State Small-Class Policies

Notably, Texas leaders addressed class-size issues in 1985 with House Bill 72, which limited class sizes in Grades K–4 to about 22 pupils. Tennessee policy persons began reducing class sizes K–3 throughout the state in 1989 with K and moved ahead, one grade per year. Other states began to follow suit, often based on STAR results. As class-size information became more available, highly visible uses of it, such as in California's voluntary statewide effort to reduce class size in elementary grades, have attracted considerable attention. California's initiative has been followed closely and described in mass media and general publications. Policy persons in other states, such as Michigan and South Carolina, have chosen to use pilot sites or to direct the limited resources for smaller classes to areas of high poverty or to schools with a high density of at-risk youth. Educators in Utah and in Nevada have taken different approaches to initiating small-class efforts, with different results. Utah has obtained quite positive outcomes and outcomes in Nevada have been inconclusive, perhaps because two key factors—rapid population growth and a shortage of space—dictated that small classes there often took the form of two teachers in large classes of more than 30 students, a condition that may be a PTR adjustment rather than a class-size effect.

Selected Class-Size Findings From STAR

What are we learning from the continuing study of class size and student outcomes? Of greatest importance, we are able to show definitively what many parents and teachers have long known: Small is better, *especially* in the early years of schooling. Better in this context seems to be much more than simply better test-score results. (Hey, home-school supporters, private school peoples, and even some education-for-pay people not only know this, they *do* small classes.) Before proceeding further, though, consider a synopsis of major class-size results from STAR and STAR-related studies. These findings obtained in long-term, experimental research are major reasons why it is time to consider class size as an important variable in student outcomes, teacher benefits, and student well-being. Here are a few not-surprising findings of STAR and STAR-related studies (Achilles, Nye, Zaharias, Fulton, & Cain, 1996, pp. 5 & 6).

- Pupils in S outperform pupils in R and RA on all cognitive measures *and* the early treatment lasts at least into Grade 8 after the K–3 start.
- Pupils in S have relatively fewer examples of poor discipline.
- The S classes seem to reduce the known deleterious effects of big schools.
- Teachers have more "on-task" time in S and this stays constant all year, but in R the behaviors decline over the year. (Tired teachers and kids. Burnout?)
- Students in S are more engaged and participative in school than are students in R and RA. This may influence staying in school to graduation.
- There are relatively fewer retentions in grade in S. This is not only better education practice, but it could save money. Grade retention is closely associated with dropouts. If so, reducing retention in grade could be very efficient.
- The traditional test-score gap between white and nonwhite pupils does not open as much in S as in R and RA classes on criterion-referenced tests. The merits of this will require serious analysis, especially in the total structure of U.S. education.
- Early identification of special needs in S seems to reduce later special education placements. (This may save *much* money for use in other ways.)
- Student scores in S are up in all tested areas, not just in targeted areas characteristic of special projects (reading and math, usually). Thus S is a broad-scale change, not a Band-Aid approach or patch on a leaky inner tube.
- Random assignment pupils (STAR R pupils) outperform non-random assigned pupils K–3 (STAR comparison-school pupils).
- It appears that instructional aides do not contribute much to pupil gains. Recall, however, that in STAR there was no special training of teachers or aides except for a small sample in

Grade 2. Training may help, but without such training, students in K–3 perform better in S than in R and better in R than in RA generally. Consider the implications of this, especially since the group that gets least benefit from RA seems to be minority males. This finding may require reconsideration given the move toward inclusion and the increase of limited-English-proficient students.

The S treatment is more *preventive* than *remedial*. If a student does not experience small classes when first entering the "system," there may be little gain without tutorials (the ultimate class size) or other expensive "treatments." This finding indicates that class-size initiatives should begin in the lowest grades and move ahead one grade at a time.

The outcomes just summarized above may seem so obvious as not to need study. Teachers, parents, and those who choose alternatives to public education for their children may intuitively know the benefits of small classes listed here, but small classes for young children are not commonly found in America's public schools. What are the elements of public perception and professional practice in education, and how is small-class research part of that practice? Many adults and policy people treat education and children with the same casual neglect that Christopher Robin shows for Winnie the Pooh. They consign education and children continuously to the same thing, but surely there is something better.

"When you wake up in the morning, Pooh," said Piglet at last, "What's the first thing you say to yourself?"

"What's for breakfast?" said Pooh. "What do you say, Piglet?"

"I say, I wonder what's going to happen exciting *today*?" said Piglet.

Pooh nodded thoughtfully. "It's the same thing," he said . . .

[Christopher Robin] gave a deep sigh, picked his bear up by the leg and walked off to the door, trailing Winnie-the-Pooh behind him. . . . and in a moment I heard Winnie-the-Pooh—bump, bump, bump—going up the stairs behind him.

(Milne, 1926, pp. 158–159)

The class-size discussion at state and federal policy levels seems serious now. Maybe we're getting around to finding a new way for Pooh to get upstairs. The following chapters explore various elements of what we know about class size, what barriers we need to hurdle to get to work on class-size adjustments, some things that need serious attention, and some speculations for the future if class-size changes are to become policy.

3

The Need
to Observe Teaching

Introduction

Studies of class size, such as Project STAR, show that students in smaller rather than larger classes generally have better outcomes or achievement, broadly defined, in several areas and not just in test scores. This small-class effect is not a new finding.

People wish to understand what occurs in small, appropriately sized classes to produce the demonstrated higher outcomes. This inquisitiveness is natural. Why or how do smaller classes improve education outcomes? Findings from well-conducted studies will add to a knowledge base for improving teacher preparation and staff development; anecdotes demonstrate specific applications of teaching and learning activities in the small classes.

As policymakers and the teachers and administrators in the "front lines" lead the newly energized efforts to get reasonably sized classes for small children in elementary schools, there are calls for understanding more about what teachers do in those small classes. A couple of definitions are repeated here to provide some common terms and guidelines about the discussion of class size and teacher practices.

1. *Class size* is the number of students regularly in a teacher's room and those for whom that teacher is responsible and accountable.

2. *Pupil–teacher ratio,* or *PTR,* is a number computed by dividing the number of students at a site (e.g., a building) by the number of professionals serving that site. PTR and class size are not synonyms. For practical purposes, and considering current legislation and practice, a "small" class has about 15–18 students per teacher and is designated in this book as 15:1, or 18:1.

According to Cahen and Filby (1979) "the search for an appropriate descriptive ratio has a long history in the research on class size. Any ratio is, at best a crude indicator ..." (p. 492). The accuracy of any computed PTR will greatly influence the results of studies that use PTR as one variable. The exact count of students in a class will vary from 15:1, and each student may influence the measured outcomes (e.g., Krueger, 1997). Thus, in reporting the research, each researcher should strive for precision in using terms such as PTR and class size.

In STAR, small classes were randomly established in the 13–17 student range. The class size and PTR in a STAR classroom might be the same, but only when that single classroom is considered. Even in STAR, when PTR is computed at the building level, the PTR for all classes (S, R and RA) is exactly the same: The class-size distinction disappears and the PTR will hide generally large classes. The example in Table 3.1 shows the PTR–class size confusion using actual STAR conditions of the experimentally established class sizes. Shadytree Elementary School, Grades K–5, has 511 students, with 252 in Grades K–2, which are shown in detail for each teacher. Grades 3–6 with three classes per grade (as in Grades 1 and 2) have 259 students and 9 teachers. Kindergarten has four STAR experimental classes with 84 students randomly assigned to two S, one R, and one RA classes.

Shadytree Elementary also houses or has the services of 9 other educators including administrator, counselor, media specialist, Title I, etc. These 9 other educators and 19 regular classroom teachers give Shadytree a PTR of 511 divided by 28 educator positions, or 18.3. Only two classes in Shadytree—the two STAR S classes in K have fewer than 18.3 students. Other classes have 9–10 more stu-

TABLE 3.1 Example of Class-Size and Pupil–Teacher Ratio (PTR) Difference. Presume Shadytree Elementary is participating in STAR. Shadytree has 252 students in Grades K–2, and a total of 511 students in K–5

Grade and Classes	Students (n)	Computation[a]
Kindergarten, $n = 84$ (STAR)		Total students, $n = 511$
Small	17	
Small	16	
Regular	25	Other educators
Regular-aide	26	Principal, $n = 1$
Grade 1, $n = 85$		Counselor, $n = 1$
A	28	Media specialist, $n = 1$
B	29	Special education, $n = 2$
C	28	Title I, $n = 2$
Grade 2, $n = 83$	27	Art, $n = .5$
A	28	Music, $n = .5$
B	28	Physical education, $n = .5$
C		Gifted, $n = \underline{.5}$
Totals (K–2)		Total "other" 9
Students	252	Total regular $\underline{19}$
Teachers	10	Total educators 28
Totals (4 and 6)		
Students	259	PTR = 511 ÷ 28 or 18.3
Teachers	9	

[a] This excludes teacher aides ($n = 4$), secretary ($n = 1$), and nurse ($n = .5$), who could add the equivalent of three more professional positions, providing a PTR of 511 ÷ 31 or 16.5.

dents than the school's PTR of 18.3, with a range of 27–29 in non-STAR classes.

In STAR schools, the R classes that served as the control group in the experiment were smaller than the classes in the rest of the grades in the school. This occurred because one guideline was that no student should have less of an education opportunity from participating in STAR than if STAR were not in that child's school. If STAR were not in Shadytree Elementary, and there were three kindergartens for the 84 students, the average class size in K would be 28. Thus, by participating in STAR and even being in the R class, a student would be in a smaller class than if STAR were not at Shadytree.

The immediate outcomes of small classes in primary grades are positive and pervasive. The benefits continue for several years, increase over the years, and are more than higher reading and math scores. Outcomes of changed PTR are not generally positive. Thus, educators need to learn more about *why* and *how* the outcomes occur in small classes. Equally important is to determine why student outcomes are not much better in changed PTR conditions. One way to improve this knowledge is by careful observations of teachers and students in small classes. Observations of teaching for research purposes can reveal what successful teachers do in small classes.

Observation for Improvement of Practice

In the practice of an art, science, or craft, people learn about improving their own performance by observing and studying what they have done, reflecting on the performance, trying again, evaluating, and improving. There are various types of observations of professional practice and many elements to focus upon in the complex classroom world.

> ... it appeared that easing these constraints (making classes smaller) allowed the teachers to do what they were already inclined to do in a better fashion.
>
> (Filby et al., 1980)

Educators can learn about class-size behaviors and outcomes through observation by collecting, comparing, and analyzing observation data. The teacher-as-researcher can learn about teaching while concurrently improving instruction. A single observation of teaching may *illustrate* something about that specific teaching effort, but collections of observations will allow the researcher to describe, define, and demonstrate *general* principles. (Quality is judged; quantity is measured.) Research done by the teacher as scholar–practitioner does not need to be complicated or highly technical, but it does require care and method. Shulman's (1988) statement about method is direct and catches up the idea of method as used here. "Method is the attribute which distinguishes research activity from mere observation and speculation" (p. 3).

☺ A school librarian in southern California said that class-size reduction increased the number of classes coming through, but that it did not pose any real problems. Instead, she and her parent-assistant found that they were able to help individual children and actually get to know the kids in each class. They could point out types of books and specific titles that would be appealing and appropriate, explaining, "If you liked that book, you'll probably like this one," or "You seem to be ready to read these chapter books in this section now." With fewer children present, there were fewer traffic jams around certain sections of shelves. There was even time left to read a story to the children.

Inquisitive people need data to resolve issues, and many seem unsatisfied with the generally theoretic idea that small classes *by themselves* lead to improved education outcomes like those in the above story. That opinion lacks data. Research says that small classes, by themselves, bring about improvements in student outcomes and in classroom practice. Disbelief of what STAR showed experimentally, that small classes, per se, lead to improved student outcomes, brings questions like the following front and center.

- If small classes by themselves bring about improved student outcomes, why does this happen?
- What do small class sizes facilitate?
- How might observation in small classes help to improve teacher preparation (preservice and in-service) for teaching in small classes?
- What things become more/less important, frequent, effective, etc. in 15:1 (smaller classes) than in 25:1 or 30:1 (larger classes)?
- Do things "cluster" or blend (mix) differently in 15:1 than in 25:1?

☺ When I got my small class, I knew *what* to do, but believed that information on *how* to get it done could help me. I knew what to do, but hadn't had a chance to do it before.

In trying to answer these types of questions, educators may rely on research in other fields, upon observations in classrooms, and upon information about schooling contexts and practices, and they may use anecdotes to illustrate their points. There are many places to begin. Stories told by practitioners may provide variables for researchers to study. Major research efforts often start from single "clinical" observations.

☺ A second-grade teacher explained that an important difference for her in small classes was in being truly able to do flexible groups. Having 20 children meant that she could sit with the kids and monitor as they participated in small-group work and partner projects. Her children this year were in their second year of being in a 20:1 class, and by December of second grade they were well ahead of last year's class in their need for phonics instruction.

☺ A second-grade teacher in southern California discovered that math instruction improved when class-size reduction began. She not only corrected papers, but took the time to analyze where mistakes were being made. She took children aside to explain ways to avoid the mistake the next time. She came to realize that she wasn't just teaching techniques, but was teaching each child.

Environmental Scan: Context Issues Such as Heating, Ventilation, and Air Conditioning (HVAC) and Space

One place to start observing classrooms is to consider space, space use, and the environment or context of the teaching–learning process. The use of space, proxemics, is one element of nonverbal communication and is important in establishing effect and affect. Space and spacing influence animal and human behavior. In a classic experiment involving a calm, nest-building fish, Tinbergen (1952) demonstrated that the stickleback would develop violent behavior—cannibalism—when its enclosed environment became crowded, even with its own kind. Calhoun's (1962) experiment showed that when the normally placid and friendly Norway rat became crowded by too many Norway rats in a defined space, a "behavioral sink" developed in which the rats demonstrated increasingly aberrant and violent behavior as they became more and more crowded. What about adults? And kids?

Sociologists, urban planners, and law enforcement persons have noticed the stressful effects of crowding on human behavior. Besides mob behavior, they have been so concerned about the negative behaviors demonstrated by humans in high-density spaces that huge high-rise public housing such as the Pruitt–Igoe development in St. Louis, Techwood in Atlanta, Jeffries Homes and Herman Gardens in Detroit, etc. have been razed. The inhabitants have been relocated in smaller communities, small housing units, or other housing situations. The gang-plagued, high-density Robert Taylor Homes in Chicago had to be destroyed because of high crime rates; officials in Baltimore and Philadelphia have destroyed large housing projects because of crime, violence, and gangs. Crowding is a force behind difficult, harmful, and illegal behavior (Hall, 1966, 1976). Crowding, by itself, causes humans to change their behaviors. Why would it be any different in classrooms? Does this idea surprise people who believe that just changing class size will change the outcomes from that class? It may seem logical that small children in primary grades need less space than the same number of adults in the same space.

☺ A teacher of a multiage classroom in southern California discovered that the space in her classroom seemed to double when class-size reduction permitted one-third fewer students. Gathering on the floor for read-aloud times meant that the children could sit on the carpet in proximity to one another and to their teacher. Conversations about books became involved and personal. She discovered that the children were listening to one

> another more and actually began responding to each
> other's comments.

Architects are adults who plan and design the use of space. Adults primarily use public space vertically and in quite stationary, predictable ways—they sit, walk, and work in the designated space. Because the space is ergometrically and scientifically large enough for adults to use and work in, architects and the adults who hire architects and develop building codes believe that the space large enough for adults is plenty large enough for kids. After all, the kids are smaller, so they need less space. Right? Wrong.

Although adults use space in very correct adult ways, kids will use the same space in very kid-like ways. "Rug rats" use space horizontally and vertically. They spread and sprawl, and the teachers of these young children need space for education: spaces for desks, learning centers, aquariums, computers, displays, toys, coats, mats. A space suitable for 25 adults who may sit in rows at desks in a classroom is much too small for 25 K–1 youngsters eager to learn.

Noise levels increase as space decreases even if the number of noisy children stays constant. Young children need quiet time; teachers need space for quiet one-on-one work with young students. The sand box, computer table, water table, and play area are all centers of activity and noise. Fewer children make less noise.

For safety reasons, state agencies may enforce regulations about classroom size, in terms of square and cubic feet, related to the number of people using the space, and about the capacity of heating, ventilating, and air-conditioning (HVAC) systems in schools. Self-contained elementary classrooms are constantly full of active bodies. Does the low-bid minimum HVAC system move enough air for a packed elementary classroom? Time after time, teachers have explained that as the day goes on, they and their students get lethargic and restless in classes with 25–30 children. Teacher and student fatigue and student misbehavior increase after lunch. In small classes, teachers often explain that they and the students feel alive, alert, and active all day long. Some of the best learning continues until the final bell. In small classes, teachers work harder but feel better.

> ☺ Reduced class size has allowed me to engage my students in more active learning activities. There is more

room and more time for dyad or small-group activities. Student's projects have improved because there are enough materials for everyone. I have enjoyed individual conferences with my students about their progress also. There is more of a "family feeling" within my class.

Observations and the comments of teachers in various-sized classes provide potential areas of inquiry about how context and environment may influence student and teacher behavior and outcomes in small classes. Observation resulting in anecdotes like those above is the first level of inquiry. The second level of inquiry may include studies of space use, measures of carbon dioxide levels as the day unfolds, and measures of sound levels and other practitioner-driven research that uses space, time, and class size as variables. Results of environmental studies may help explain both academic gains and behavior benefits in small classes. Space and class size can be variables in studies such as the following.

1. Teacher use of space; student use of space

   - "Rug rats": vertical vs. horizontal use of space
   - Required space for learning centers, etc. for primary students
   - Crowding effects on behavior: student discipline, lethargy, possessiveness
   - A key space question: What are the space possibilities for small classes *other than* traditional classrooms?

2. Space as a function of student behavior: sharing, territoriality, turf
3. Space and class size as factors in fatigue and air quality throughout a day
4. Noise levels and space, class size, learning outcomes, learning centers, etc.

Types of Observation

By following uncomplicated but careful procedures, the teacher as scholar–practitioner can provide important insights into teaching and learning in classrooms. The observations can be unstructured or structured, formal or informal, but they should be made by following reasonable care and method. Some observations are very detailed, relying upon scripting or counting events every so many seconds. In these "low-inference" observations, the observer has only to count, categorize, and report the data. "High-inference" observations usually are general and qualitative. The observer constructs meaning from what is observed, and may ask the teacher or person being observed to explain or add meaning to what the observer saw. In a class of 14 males and 14 females, a low-inference observation might be that the teacher initiated communications 20 times with the males and 40 times with the females in one 40-minute class period: The females received twice as many teacher-initiated communication events as did the males (a quantitative statement). The high-inference observer might note that the teacher preferred to communicate with the females, or even was prejudiced toward males in a classroom setting.

A combination of low- and high-inference observations provides productive, valid, and reliable information about teaching and learning in classroom settings, especially when the observations are supported by data on student outcomes. An example of a simple observation process is provided in the following section.

A Sample of Observation Processes (Unstructured)

When people discuss "observation" in education, they usually think about an administrator, supervisor, or peer watching someone else teaching, perhaps for evaluative purposes. However, an educator really can observe his or her own teaching, too. This can be done in two ways: (a) by watching a video of one's own performance and (b) by being acutely aware of what is going on and reflecting upon the business of teaching. A teacher might ask a colleague to observe, critique, and discuss his or her teaching. In either case, there should be some way to collect and categorize the events that are observed to help the individual understand what has been observed.

Each set of observations represents unique information about the teaching of an individual teacher at the time of observation. Using common categories for classifying the teaching behaviors of several teachers in some format—even by content analysis or just

TABLE 3.2 Sample Nominal Sorting of Teacher Behavior in Five Classes

	Teacher or Observation Set					
Behavior	*A*	*B*	*C*	*D*	*E*	*Totals*
1	X	—	—	X	—	2
2	X	X	X	—	X	4
3	X	X	X	X	X	5
4	X	X	X	X	X	5
5	X	X	X	X	X	5
6	—	—	X	X	X	3
7	X	X	—	—	—	2
8	X	—	—	X	—	2
9	X	X	—	X	—	3
10	—	X	—	—	—	1
Total (of 10)	8	7	5	7	5	32
Students (Total)	14	16	24	16	26	96
M	7	7	10	9	14	47
F	7	9	14	7	12	49

Duration: Approximately 30 minutes per classroom.
Day: Wednesday, 9/19/99; *Time*: 11 AM – 1 PM.
Activity: Language Arts.

seeking out categories that seem descriptive of teaching events—can provide a summary of several sets of observations to show similarities and also to identify unique cases. Consider the example in Table 3.2 where only the frequency of behavior is reported. No description of a behavior and no judgment about the value or quality of any behavior are stated or implied. When only the frequency of an observed event is recorded, the observer is using low-inference methods. Analysis of the recorded events can provide important insights, questions, and qualitative estimates of the behaviors.

Of the 10 different behaviors observed in this single comparison, all 5 teachers used behaviors 3, 4, and 5. Were these "core" behaviors? Only teacher B used behavior 10. Was behavior 10 "good" or "poor" teaching? If an observer analyzed behaviors of additional teachers, or even behaviors of the same teachers several more times, a "picture" of classroom events would begin to form, or a trend or pattern might become evident.

What can you see in a single set of data? What added information might you obtain if you repeated the observations, or if you expanded your inquiry? Try this brief exercise.

Using only the data in Table 3.2, including the context information about numbers of students by sex, subject area, etc., begin to ask questions or to draw inferences based on the data available. What other information might you derive from interviews with the teachers? What questions or interpretations can you add from your knowledge of professional practice?

Figure 3.1. Exercise on Interpreting Classroom Observation

Behavior 10 was used only by teacher B, and used only once during the observation period. It may have related to some unique classroom event, such as a teacher responding to a student's personal problem. Teachers C and E both had only 5 behaviors recorded. Teachers A, B, and D averaged 7.3 behaviors in the same duration. Teachers C and E have about 25 students and Teachers A, B, and D have about 15 students. Might the number of students in a classroom influence the range and amount of a teacher's teaching behaviors?

Summary

This chapter has suggested that context may influence the small-class outcomes. Context variables such as space use, crowding, and even environmental factors such as air quality may influence teacher and pupil classroom behaviors. An example of the major confusion possible if PTR and class size are not clearly defined points to another variable that can be isolated in observation studies where students can be counted.

Chapter 4 includes results of some observation studies in classrooms and also summarizes teacher comments about and perceptions of teaching in large and in small classes.

4

What Happens in
Various-Sized Classes

In 1979, just one year after Glass and Smith (1978) developed their curve or graph of the relationship between class size and student academic achievement, Cahen and Filby (1979) noted that Glass and Smith did not make

> any attempt to see how this relationship is conditioned by a set of variables we shall call quality of instruction. It would be useful to find out whether, and how, good and poor teaching or environmental conditions alter the curve. (p. 493)

Questions that Cahen and Filby posed are still awaiting answers today. Are the curriculum and the actual test that measures outcomes variables, too? Even though the research shows that class size, per se, influences student outcomes positively, the variables of good or poor teaching, of environment or context (other than class size), and of curriculum or content will possibly change the positive benefits of class size.

Cahen and Filby described a field study in process at that time to try to determine what teachers did differently in small and in large classes. In that study, two regular second-grade classes were established. At mid-year, a third teacher received students from each class, making three small classes, each taught by one teacher. Researchers and the teachers studied the classes to find out what was different. This study was important because, as Cahen and Filby noted, "many people have suggested that reducing class size will have no effect if teachers do exactly the same thing in a small class as in a large one" (p. 494). In the 1990s this same idea continues to be reflected in the comment that students would learn more in a large class with a good teacher than in a small class with a poor teacher. Myth, tradition, and folklore persist. Research has substantiated a class-size effect and people know exactly what to do to get the effect—just reduce the class size. Obtaining a class-size effect is administratively mutable. There is far less certitude on exactly what makes a good teacher and less is known about exactly how to make a good teacher better either through preservice or in-service training. Thus, a logical question might be "How much more will students learn with a good teacher in a small class than with that same good teacher in a large class?"

Part of the results of the field study just described appear below. Teachers in that study did pretty much the same things in the small and in the large-class conditions. What did change was the quantity and the quality of what they were doing before the class-size change. In the small class they could introduce more topics, cover more content, or use more individual teaching strategies. Most "changes" were only modifications of existing processes, and not radical or new approaches.

> The teachers welcomed the opportunity for greater *individualization of instruction. Changes in curriculum also occurred,* most in the form of enrichment activities such as more instructional games, reading for pleasure, and field trips. Within the basic reading and mathematics curriculum, some teachers found that students completed lessons and progressed through the curriculum more quickly. Other teachers developed lessons in greater depth. *While the teachers expressed a sense of greater freedom from the constraints imposed by a large class and increased enthusiasm, it appeared that easing these constraints allowed the teachers to do what they were already inclined to do in a better fashion. Most of the changes could*

*be described as modifications or improvements within the teachers'
existing styles and plans of instruction* (emphasis added).

(ERIC-CEM, 1994, Abstract ED 219365)

The Filby et al. (1980) conclusion about teaching in small classes
is reinforced by the materials in the next sections.

Environmental Conditions: Class Size as Context

The most readily evident change in the environmental conditions
that Cahen and Filby ask about is the class size itself. This is a true
observed difference. A class-size change does "alter the curve" defined by Glass and Smith (1978), and also by Bloom (1984a, b). The
class itself is an environment for the teacher, for each student, and
for groups of students. The classroom is the context for the class, including the teacher. This is the very reason that STAR researchers
collected data on individual students, but used the classroom—the
class average—as the unit of analysis. Each student in the class is
not an independent measure, but is dependent upon peers, teachers,
context, and content of the classroom.

Holding time of day, available materials, and space, that is,
square (or cubic) footage of the classroom, constant, a class-size reduction from 30 students and one teacher (30:1) to 15:1 immediately influences environmental variables such as space and fresh air
per occupant, crowdedness, materials per pupil, noise levels, and
teacher time for each student. Research has shown that space (e.g.,
intimate, private, personal, and public space) and space relationships influence animal behavior, including human behavior (Hall,
1966). In the change from 30:1 to 15:1, each student has about twice
as much space (material or toys, too) and potentially twice as much
individual teacher time in 15:1 as in 30:1: Noise levels, air quality,
use of diverse teaching stations, etc. will be improved in 15:1 classes,
and these environmental conditions, brought about with no effort
other than small classes, will influence student outcomes.

☺ A second-grade teacher explained that although her
class this past year had a reputation as the "class from
hell," she's been far more able to deal with problems.

> Relationships are closer. There are fewer arguments and
> more warmer feelings coupled with genuine friendships
> with parents and children. As she explained, "I always
> feel a bit sad when it's time to say good-bye in June. This
> year I felt like crying."

Results of Some Observations of Small-Class Teaching

The following tables show results of observations conducted in small classes, or comparisons of observations in smaller and in larger classes. The text offers an initial summary of those observations. Figure 4.1 is a synopsis of early classroom observations done by Olson, as reported by Cavenaugh (1994) in *Educational Alternatives*. Figure 4.2 includes a listing of teacher behaviors and resultant student benefits from Project SAGE (Student Achievement Guarantee in Education) in Wisconsin (Molnar, 1998). Figure 4.3 shows some small-class benefits compiled by Cooper (1989), based primarily on earlier reviews and composed prior to the availability of STAR results.

Oak Hill Elementary, High Point, North Carolina undertook "Project Success." The class size was based on 15:1 with no full-time teacher assistant and a teacher agreement to teach using more hands-on learning strategies and to teach for higher-level thinking. Four Grade 1 teachers provided information about teaching in classes of 15 and of 26 students. After the same teachers had taught in both 15:1 and 26:1 settings, Jean Owen, Ed.D., Oak Hill principal, interviewed the teachers and summarized their comments (Table 4.1).

Several researchers have synthesized benefits of a teacher having small class sizes. The consistency of the findings across the studies will not surprise any teacher, parent, or administrator who has taught or been in schools and observed children closely or who has thought seriously about small classes. Olson's succinct comparisons (shown in Fig. 4.1, as cited in Cavenaugh, 1994), which are divided into teacher and student benefits, really encapsulate results shown in Figures 4.2 and 4.3, also. The division into student and teacher benefits makes clear the reciprocal and similar benefits for both students and teachers, hardly surprising if they were in the same rooms at the same time and if teaching and learning are reciprocal events.

1. Teachers employ a wider variety of instructional strategies, methods, and learning activities, and are more effective with them.
2. Teacher attitudes and morale are more positive.
3. Classroom management and discipline are better.
4. Students benefit from more individual instruction.
5. Students develop better human relations and have greater regard for others.
6. Students learn the basic skills better and master more subject matter content.
7. Students engage in more creative and divergent thinking processes.
8. Students learn how to function more effectively as members and leaders of groups of varying sizes and purposes.
9. Student attitudes and perceptions are more positive.

Source: Dr. Martin Olson

Figure 4.1. Nine Defensible Generalizations About Class Size When Teachers Have Fewer Rather Than More Students. (From Cavenaugh, 1994. Dr. Martin Olson's breakthrough study in the United States nearly 30 years ago focused on the impact of different class size groupings.)

Olson's results illustrate possible reasons why class-size research shows many class-size effects for student outcomes, and why the focus upon test-score achievement vastly understates the value of small classes. Olson's summary shows positive cognitive, behavior, and affective outcomes: improved test results, improved behavior, and improved attitudes. Olson described complementary benefits for teachers and for students. Teacher and student attitudes improve in small classes. Teachers report that in small classes, discipline is better, and classroom management is less troublesome, but these positive teacher perceptions are undoubtedly the reciprocal of students who work comfortably in groups and display good human relations skills. Teachers and students help each other. The classroom climate changes.

The narratives in Figure 4.2 express observations of Project SAGE evaluators. The refrain is now familiar: Better classroom man-

In their qualitative research, evaluators found that in SAGE classrooms,

1. Little time is required to manage the class or to deal with discipline problems;*
2. Much time is spent on instruction, actively teaching;*
3. A large portion of instruction is individualized and spent in diagnosing student needs, providing help, and in monitoring progress; and
4. Students showed increases in "on task" and "active learning" behaviors over the year.* These behaviors were also found to be related to SAGE student performance on the CTBS.

In general, the first-year SAGE results appear to be tracking the results of the STAR study.

Figure 4.2. Findings on Teaching Characteristics in Small Classes in Project SAGE (Molnar, 1998, p. 37). The findings denoted by asterisks are like the increase in time-on-task found in Success Starts Small in North Carolina.

agement, active instruction, individual attention, and lots of time on task (Molnar, 1998). These four areas describe what research, theory, and exemplary practice have shown to be important for improved student test-score performance. SAGE small-class students achieved better than did their large-class comparison groups.

Cooper (1989) divided small-class benefits into nonachievement and achievement outcomes. His portrayals strengthen the idea that small classes are not just production centers for higher test outcomes. Although Figure 4.3 lists the differences as teacher benefits, there is hand-in-glove correspondence between improved teacher outcomes such as morale and attitude and what teachers are able to do— individualization, positive class climate, and so on.

One way to find out what teachers say about differences that they perceive in classes of 15:1 and 25:1 is to interview teachers who have taught in both settings. Because small classes are the change that educators are striving toward, such as the California Class-Size Reduction (CSR) effort, most interviewers would ask teachers how current small classes differ from prior large classes. Many stories

Nonachievement Variables (That May Affect Achievement)
(25 of 30 Comparisons Favored Small)

A. TEACHER VARIABLES (in small classes): There was

- Higher teacher morale
- Improved attitude toward students
- Satisfaction with performance is better

B. INSTRUCTION (in small classes): There was

- More individualization and informality
- Higher quality instruction
- Positive climate

Figure 4.3. Summary and Paraphrase of Teacher Benefits (from Cooper, 1989, pp. 85–87). Cooper cited key meta-analyses and other studies in deriving the conclusion; for example, Glass and Smith (1978), Educational Research Service (1978, 1980), and Glass et al. (1982). These prior findings from meta-analyses and reviews were obtained later in STAR and STAR-related studies (e.g., SSS study in NC).

throughout this text have that time orientation. Project Success reversed the expected time sequence. Teachers there commented on teaching in small classes while teaching large classes *after* their small-class experiences. The small-class to large-class "before–after" stories from Project Success are, on the one hand, refreshing, because they reverse the usual large-to-small shift, but also saddening because they represent a move away from the desired outcomes of schooling. The reader can feel the teacher frustration and hurt, all-too-common feelings of many teachers when they are unable to reach each child.

Table 4.1 displays the before–after teacher comments divided into two sections. Section A has 17 entries about teaching in small classes. Overwhelmingly, these statements are characterized by "more," not by "different"—unless the definition of different includes more of the same. And it might. "More" suggests some cor-

TABLE 4.1 Project Success—Progress Report (3/17/93)

A. Immediate Observable Outcomes of Class Size of 15

1. More individual attention
2. More personal space for each student
3. More personal teacher–student conversations
4. More time to diagnose how the students are thinking and to determine their understandings and misunderstandings
5. More time to diagnose and develop their most successful learning style
6. More time to get to know each student and their families— a message to parents that the teacher really cares because she/he knows all about us
7. More time for students to get to know each other
8. More time for the teacher to develop a sense of community among classmates, connect her/his students with other big sister/big brother classes in the school
9. More students reading on more advanced levels
10. More students understanding math concepts, not simply writing numbers and number facts
11. All students participating in "seminars" discussing literature on their level, making concept connections, and thinking about human values
12. More self-confidence for learning regardless of abilities
13. Wider range of abilities able to learn together (fewer referrals out during these critical early years)
14. More time and space to develop hands-on/student-initiated learning rather than relying on mostly didactic, teacher-controlled learning
15. More time to give "troubled kids" the attention they so desperately need, reducing greatly the likelihood of their becoming discipline problems
16. More energy for collegial planning that led to well thought out, creative "webbing" thematic lessons
17. A sense of peacefulness in the class

TABLE 4.1 (Continued)

B. Immediate Observable Outcomes of Class Size of 24

1. I cannot meet all subject needs daily.
2. I used to have daily reading conferences. Now I read individually with each child about two times weekly.
3. I feel frustrated that in the critical first-grade year, I cannot assess their reading individually and specify the focus they need.
4. They used to read to me every day. They still want to, and it seems to hurt their feelings if they can't.
5. This at-risk population needs daily help. I want to give that help but can't get to them as often as they need.
6. I don't know the children as well.
7. During each lesson now, each child does not get to answer. Last year, each child answered three and four times in each lesson.
8. Lessons are 15 to 25 minutes longer as I check all children. I do more "up front" teaching. This leaves little time for students to do the independent exploratory learning and thinking.
9. There are more student conflicts in the classroom.
10. There is less space for each child.
11. I have to move on before all students have learned. Last year I could make sure every child did and learned what he or she was supposed to.
12. Students do not present their work orally as much. Oral communication is a major need, but the class size keeps us from doing it as much.

---

responding "less." Maybe the "less" is fewer of the poor teaching practices. Does the new "more–less" mix provide a different learning environment?

Section B of Table 4.1 includes 12 entries about teaching in classes of 24–25 students. Overwhelmingly, these teacher observations reflect frustration, reduction of positive teaching efforts, less individual attention, and fewer student productions. Differences expressed in these two lists tell their own story of quality teaching.

Themes reported in Figures 4.1 through 4.3 and in Table 4.1 reinforce each other. Teachers in small classes consistently report doing what they believe will help students learn. Observers have confirmed that in small classes teachers do more of what they already know to do. Teacher self-reports may also include more wish than fact about teaching differently. Researchers have reported fewer *observed* differences or changes than teachers themselves report (e.g., Filby et al., 1980; Shapson et al., 1980). How does this idea play out? The next section presents teacher behaviors that were collected by observing teachers in small and in large classes.

> ☺ The lower class size has been very rewarding for me this year. I can meet student needs better and believe that I know my students better individually. There is a marked decrease in discipline problems in the small classes; the group members are very nurturing and supportive of one another's needs. Students seem to take on more personal responsibility for the class.

A Structured Observation Study:
Success Starts Small (SSS)

In 1993–1994 we conducted a year-long observation study of teaching behaviors of teachers in small classes ("Life in a Small Class" or "Success Starts Small") and of teaching behaviors of teachers in classes of about 24 students or 24:1. The small classes had about 14 students (14:1) (Achilles et al., 1994; Kiser-Kling, 1995). We observed in two schools selected because they were nearly identical on key variables (school size, student race, SES, prior-year student performance, teacher experience, etc.). Both sites had schoolwide Title I funds. School A had small classes, and school B used a traditional approach to deliver Title I services through projects and pull-out activities.

Two graduate students, who had four and eight years of experience in primary teaching, and one professor observed the teachers and recorded results on an instrument called the PIT (French & Galloway, nd). The PIT allowed researchers to sort *teacher* behaviors into categories called personal (P), institutional (I), and task (T) communications, and a category called mixed (M). Most recorded behaviors were T, or task, that described "time-on-task" in the classroom. The next highest category was I or institutional behaviors that describe "playing school"—lining up, discipline, transitions, classroom management. We recorded behaviors about every 5–7 seconds for snapshots of 10–20 minutes of class interactions after we had established interrater agreements (over 90% for this study). We observed teachers teaching the same subjects, at about the same time of day and year (fall to spring) and collected about 8000 samples of teacher behaviors. Observations were made primarily in Grade-1 classrooms (four rooms of 14:1 and two rooms of 24:1) and secondarily for context in K and Grade-2 classrooms in both schools. We aggregated the observations from the single teachers into the two groups of interest: teachers in small (14:1) and in larger (24:1) classes. Then we compared behaviors of teachers and outcomes of students in the two groups.

In addition to classroom observations, we collected context information, such as room size, use of aides or/and volunteers, grouping for instruction, referrals to the office for discipline, etc. As a standard outcome measure and to meet Title I requirements, we obtained pre- (fall, 1993) and posttest (spring, 1994) matched-pair score data for students in Grade 1. Students in both schools had experienced kindergarten or similar pre-school time.

As shown in Figures 4.4 and 4.5, teachers in both large and small classes started the school year with about the same amount of on-task behaviors. As the year progressed, the average time on task (the T behaviors in the PIT system) changed in the different-sized classrooms. Teachers in large classes decreased the percentage of on-task behaviors and teachers in small classes increased their percentage of on-task behaviors between October and April, both in the target first grades (Fig. 4.4) and in the K and Grade-2 classes throughout the two schools (Fig. 4.5). Students in the small classes outperformed students in large classes on pre- to posttest-score gains ($p \leq .01$) on matched-pair analyses and reduced their discipline problems by one-half as they experienced the small classes. From these fairly low-inference data, the researchers and teachers constructed explanations and hypothesized connections that could be the objects of future research.

Information and inferences can be developed from each data set provided in Figure 4.4 or in Figure 4.5, or by considering the data

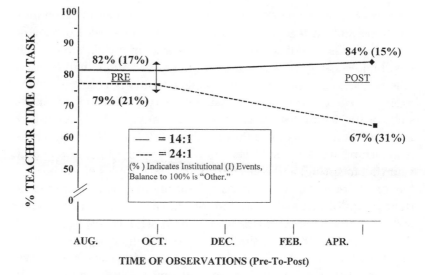

Figure 4.4. Teacher Time-on-Task in Two First-Grade Class Conditions: (14:1 and 24:1). (From Kiser-Kling, 1995, p. 64, Table 15.)

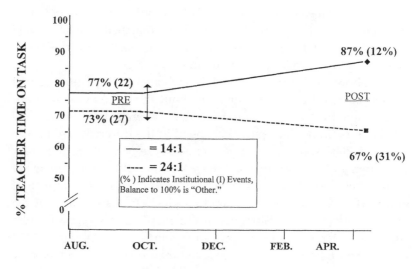

Figure 4.5. Approximate Teacher Time-on-Task in Two Class Conditions: (14:1 and 24:1), School Level K–3. (From Achilles et al., 1994, and Kiser-Kling, 1995.)

together. From modest clinical observation such as this, a researcher can design studies that may lead to clearer understandings of why students in smaller classes generally outperform students in larger classes.

Findings from the SSS study, either in comparisons between classes of 24:1 and 14:1 in matched buildings or in comparisons of 14:1 (1994) with 24:1 (1992 and 1993) in the same building (Project Success, Table 4.1), show positive observation, test-score, and behavior differences, favoring students and teachers in 1:14 over 1:24 class settings. Details of student benefits from SSS and from other studies are in Chapter 6.

Small Class Lessons From Burke County Teachers

Burke County, North Carolina, educators began small classes on a pilot basis and then expanded the program so all students in Grades 1–3 were in classes of 16–18 students per teacher. Over the years of the small-class implementation, the teachers have worked together and shared successful teaching practices. The small numbers of students in each class let teachers individualize instruction and use student portfolios as a teaching strategy, gave them a way to monitor student performance and growth, and were a centerpiece for involving parents. A discussion of the teacher uses of the portfolio process in Burke County shows how the teachers perceive that small classes facilitate improved teaching and learning.

In a small-class setting the teacher has time and space to teach well. Small classes trigger changes in *categories* of schooling activities. In small classes, teachers can expect the following positive outcomes in classroom management, parent interest in school, and in curriculum and instruction (data from Burke County teachers).

Selected Positive Aspects of Teaching in 16:1 Classes

- Teachers can individualize programs for students on their levels.
- Reading instruction is more varied and successful.
- Increased time-on-task, including strategies such as

    – Individual reading time, daily

    – Reading logs, with time to monitor student growth

    – Accelerated reader program

    – "Book Buddies"

- Teachers can monitor and use volunteers well.
- Teachers can bond with each student and increase one-on-one student contact.
- There are greater expectations *and* accountability at all levels.

Parents in School Increase and Improve

- There is high attendance at parent conferences and at parent meetings, such as at report card pickup.
- Teachers send newsletters (each teacher sends home newsletters 3–5 times each marking period).
- Parental involvement increases in classrooms, often as volunteers.
- Parent-Teacher Organization (PTO) attendance increases.
- Pupil self-esteem is elevated by the "community" atmosphere in rooms.

Classroom Management

- There are many fewer behavior problems in small classes.
- There are stronger peer relations in small classes.
- Classroom environment and space are safe and conducive to learning.
- Small-group instruction is more manageable than in larger classes.

Changes or Increases in Curriculum and Instruction

- Frequent individual reading and writing conferences are possible.
- Students enjoy more hands-on activities, especially in math and science.
- Teachers can use programs and inventories to monitor students' active learning.

- There are observable increases in computer lab/media interest and use.
- Small classes establish a pattern of early success in school.
- Added portfolio use improves the alternative and authentic assessment of student growth.

The Portfolio Process: An Example of a Small-Class Benefit

When used properly, the portfolio process is time-consuming and individual-intensive. In a small class, a teacher can use a portfolio not only to collect and display student work, but also as a teaching tool and communication bridge with family and home. Small classes afford the time and the space for working on and storing portfolios. The portfolio process is an important part of instruction in the Burke County schools. Several teachers from Hillcrest Elementary shared ideas about using portfolios in a small class.

Basic Steps to Portfolio Assessment

- Decide what language arts and other competencies are most important to you and to your students.
- Determine specific tasks to demonstrate the important competencies.
- Define standards of student performance.
- Implement a method for managing the portfolios.
- Evaluate the portfolios at regular intervals, jointly with students and parents.

What Do Students Include in Their Portfolios?

In general, a student portfolio can contain what the student chooses. The portfolio should include work samples that show student progress in basic skills and in development of higher-order thinking skills. The small-class setting affords the student and teacher time to establish two portfolios, if they choose, or at least to divide one portfolio into two major sections: the process or working folio and the product or "showcase" folio.

Selection of material for a portfolio can be open-ended, limited only by the physical dimensions of the portfolio and storage constraints, and time to determine "the rules" with the students. Portfolio contents used successfully in small classes include:

- Questions, issues, brainstorming, notes associated with research projects
- Sketches, semantic maps, photographs
- Writing samples, rough drafts, works in progress, published "books"
- Peer and teacher feedback, and student reflection on this feedback
- Lists of books read and student comments about the books
- Lists of those with whom the student shared the books
- Audiotapes of the student reading: Perhaps the student will record readings once a month or so; include the student's self-evaluation of the reading
- Student personal reactions to classroom experiences and self-evaluations

What's in a Process or Working Folio? (Samples)

- Student-maintained chronological index
- A range of work for specific purposes and audiences
- Student writing in all stages: notes, daily journals, drafts, etc.
- Drawings, art projects, sketches
- Questionnaires, interviews with students, checklists of learning outcomes
- Anecdotal records from observations of students working in groups or individually
- Teacher feedback and parent responses to student work

What's in a Product or "Showcase" Folio? (Samples)

- Autobiography of a writer
- "Biography" of a work, from prewriting to final draft
- Special projects or end-of-year exhibitions
- List of recreational reading for the year
- Reflective pieces about growth and challenges

- Best work so far in reading, writing, math, and other content areas
- Most challenging work
- An enjoyable *learning* experience; free-choice items

Suggestions for Classroom Management of Portfolios

- Treat each portfolio as a valuable item *belonging to the student.*
- Require students to take responsibility for their portfolios. Have them make portfolio entries and maintain an up-to-date list of contents.
- Have the students select some items, generally ones that "show how well you can do." The teacher will choose others, which represent either the student's best work or at least typical performance. Occasionally, pick items together, discussing why or why not to include particular pieces of work.

Encourage each student to review the portfolio regularly and to think about personal growth and achievement. A student "portfolio self-evaluation" worksheet (see Table 4.2) will help a student to maintain a portfolio and can guide reviews of a student's work during parent–teacher–student conferences.

Small Classes Let Individualization Happen

Teachers are increasingly using portfolios in versatile ways other than only for alternative assessments. Teachers use them to diversify instruction and often as the focal point for parent–student–teacher meetings. The creative use of student work and the structured involvement of parents to help assess student progress strengthen home and school ties so parents can help with the education process.

With a class of 28–30 children, many aspects of good teaching portrayed in the discussion of portfolio use are difficult or impossible to manage. Individual attention is at the heart of instruction. Whether a teacher uses portfolios or some other individualization process, the small class makes teaching and learning a meaningful and productive event; large classes hinder teachers from doing what they know how to do.

TABLE 4.2 Sample of a Portfolio Self-Evaluation Form

Name_____Date_____

PORTFOLIO SELF-EVALUATION

1. Put your best portfolio piece on top in your folder. What makes this your best piece?

   _____

   _____

2. List some other items that your portfolio contains:

   _____

   _____

3. Overall would you say that your portfolio contains your best work? Yes___ No___ Why? Why not?

   _____

   _____

4. If you could start over, how might you work differently on your portfolio?

   _____

   _____

5. What letter grade would you give for your portfolio?_____
   Why?_____

   _____

6. What goal for your portfolio will you set for next quarter?

   _____

   _____

Summary and Conclusions

Bain, Achilles, Zaharias, and McKenna (1992) summarized advantages of the small-class condition as told by the teachers in Project STAR. That summary expresses the general differences that teachers find between teaching in larger and in smaller classes. The class-size "differences" they expressed are really more of the same. Is "more" different?

A common benefit cited by teachers in small and regular-plus-aide classes was that they were better able to individualize instruction. These teachers reported increased monitoring of student behavior and learning, opportunities for more immediate and more individualized reteaching, more enrichment, more frequent interactions with each child, a better match between each child's ability and the instructional opportunities provided, a more detailed knowledge of each child's needs as a learner, and more time to meet individual learners' needs using a variety of instructional approaches. (Bain et al., 1992, p. 254)

The teacher comments about benefits and outcomes of a small class tell a story of teachers being able to teach and to do what successful teachers in STAR and in SAGE and in Olson's review all did: provide individual attention, work with each child, use the advantages of space, and the opportunity to work with troubled students. Statistically higher test scores, fewer discipline cases sent to the office, improved parent relations, and other indicators confirmed teacher-expressed benefits.

A major reason for the achievement gain found in small classes is clearly the increase in time-on-task (the PIT category designated as T) in 15:1 classes from about 80% in the fall to about 88% in the spring. Teacher time-on-task in classes of 24:1 declined from about 80% in the fall to about 65% in the spring, at the very time that the students were tested. The observers noted that this time-on-task difference translated into a purposeful, busy but calm classroom of 14:1—Project Success teachers reported a "sense of peacefulness in the class"—when compared to a hectic, frustrating class as teachers in 24:1 tried to rush students to learn the basics for upcoming tests. In the 14:1 classes, teachers had already ascertained that their students were prepared for the tests, so they could use time for enrichment or review, absent the pressure to cover more material at the last minute. The tone or climate in the classes of 24:1 was harried and hurried; in the classes of 14:1 it was calm and focused.

☺ The mutual respect between students and teacher was stronger than I have ever seen it. My students showed very positive gains in academics and in their computer skills. I was pleased to have more "quality" time to spend

> with my low achievers, as well as with my high achiev-
> ers. Discipline problems were nonexistent. Students and
> teachers loved the small classes.

Teachers in North Carolina told the same stories over and over. At a workshop on small-class instruction held in June 1998, teachers of small classes reported on what they believed were small-class benefits. The consistency of their responses serves as an estimate of reliability not only internally for this group, but also externally when compared to results of studies and anecdotes from small-class teachers in other states.

☺ "The main advantage is being able to work one-to-one with more students. It helps maintain better discipline and students work as a family unit."

☺ "With fewer students, I can get to know a students' weaknesses and strengths quickly, and begin to address them."

☺ "More individual help to students:

- More personal relationships
- Can build self-esteem
- Improved discipline
- More time for fun learning activities"

☺ "More time for individual help:

- More opportunity to use technology
- More time for communication with parents about their child's progress
- Peer tutoring"

☺ "Small-class size enables me to get to know each student better and to provide for the individual needs of the students."

☺ "Smaller classes for me have provided important benefits:

- Closer personal relationship with students/parents
- More time for individual help
- Time for whole-group, small-group, and individual reading classes"

☺ "Small classes allow me much more time for working with small groups and particularly for working closely with the students who require individualized instruction and individual attention."

☺ "Behavior is better in the small class. You don't have as many kids to work off each other."

The stories of teachers of small classes today express just what reviews of early class-size studies found. Observations and quantitative data agree. Let's get on with it!

Lessons Learned
From Small Classes

Project STAR (Student/Teacher Achievement Ratio), a
study of the educational effects of class size in the state
of Tennessee (Word et al., 1990) is one of the great experiments in education in U.S. history.

(Mosteller, Light, & Sachs, 1996, p. 814)

Lessons From STAR: Introduction

Although Project STAR is probably best known for its experimental
nature and the resultant analyses of student academic achievement,
the longitudinal study contained much more than test-score analyses. Throughout STAR's duration, researchers visited and observed
in schools, interviewed teachers and administrators, discussed results, and prepared and presented research papers on a variety of
topics not specifically related to test performance of students.

How and why class size might have caused the positive achievement-test gains demonstrated by students in STAR's small classes intrigued the STAR researchers. *The STAR Final Report* (Word et al., 1990) contains several sections devoted to this issue: "Teacher Effectiveness," "Training," "Effects of Class Size on Classroom Processes," and Appendix D, "Teacher Effectiveness Findings." Individual STAR researchers have analyzed what occurred in classrooms containing different numbers of students. Some studies were based primarily on observations in the classrooms (e.g., Evertson & Folger, 1989; Evertson & Randolph, 1989). In other studies, researchers analyzed samples of the nearly 1100 interviews conducted with teachers participating in STAR from 1985 through 1989 (Bain et al., 1992; Johnston, 1990), or followed up long-range differences in groups of students who started school in different-sized classes (e.g., Bain, Zaharias, Cain, Word, & Binkley, 1997).

Teacher Behavior Derived From Studies of Training in STAR

Evertson and Folger (1989) reported the effects of in-service training for a subsample of STAR second-grade teachers conducted during the third year of STAR. In determining the effects of training, researchers observed teacher and student behaviors in all three of STAR's class types (S, R, RA), and related training to year-end student academic outcomes. Differences that researchers observed are important in understanding why students in S outperformed students in other class types. As the researchers reported,

> There are predictable differences in class processes that follow simply from the numbers: students are more visible; each student is more likely to get a turn more often during class lessons; students don't have to wait as long for help; students initiate more contacts with teachers. (Evertson & Folger, 1989, p. 10)

Of special note, Evertson and Folger determined that although the time spent in class activities and lesson formats did not vary by class size in most subjects, teachers in small classes averaged 64 minutes a day on reading and teachers in regular classes averaged 84 minutes. Teachers in S spent 20 minutes less per day on reading lessons than did teachers in R and RA classes, but students in S had significantly higher reading scores than did their peers in R and RA. Think what a good teacher can do with 20 minutes "extra" each day (180 days × 20 is 3600 minutes, or 60 hours per year).

Teachers and students in small classes spent 20 minutes less per day on reading lessons than did teachers in larger classes, but the students in small classes had significantly higher reading scores than did their peers in the large classes.

Evertson and Randolph (1989) found that teachers in S did essentially the same things as did teachers in large classes. They divided classes into groups. They used the same methods and lessons. Teachers adhered to "tried-and-true" methods (Evertson & Randolph, 1989, p. 98), so one presumes that they considered those methods useful or had found them beneficial in the past.

In discussing their findings, Evertson and Randolph identified two important conditions that they noted in the different class types: curriculum and measurement. The curriculum in all classes in Grades K–3 in Tennessee during STAR was tightly aligned to achievement of basic skills that could be readily measured by standardized and curriculum-driven, criterion-referenced tests. These were the objectives on the state Basic Skills First (BSF) criterion-referenced test. The researchers noted, "Where this type of recall-oriented performance is closely linked to what will be tested, there may be no need or encouragement for teachers to change" (Evertson & Randolph, 1989, p. 101). Evertson and Randolph (1989, p. 102) connected the idea of teaching for specific skills to the "factory metaphor" of education in which the teacher as supervisor of students as workers emphasizes "doing work" and completing assignments "rather than on learning and applying concepts."

Here is yet another question for researchers to consider. How do concepts or metaphors of school, measurement processes, and an emphasis on learning or academic outcomes that are the easily measured "basics" influence what teachers might do to help students attain higher measurable outcomes? Do the curriculum and the measurement processes influence to a large degree other important elements of the learning environment, even to narrowing the range of teacher options?

The material presented by Evertson and Folger (1989) and by Evertson and Randolph (1989) using a subsample of STAR teachers tracks closely with results from studies presented in Chapter 4 about teaching in a small class. Essentially, teachers in small classes did pretty much what they had been doing in their larger classes. Researcher-observed differences of classroom practices in larger and smaller classes seem to emphasize the numbers of students in the classes, and not specific staff development issues.

A STAR finding that supports many other studies of teaching practices in classes of differing sizes was that teacher in-service training as conducted in STAR with a subsample of teachers did not improve student achievement (Word et al., 1990, p. 192). There are several possible reasons for these findings. One reason, discussed in detail elsewhere, is that small-class effects are more pronounced in early grades when the student enters school, so a Grade-2 effort is too late. A second reason could be that the training was not useful or used. Third, perhaps the outcome measure, test scores, is not sensitive to teacher training. A fourth reason, one not popular with the staff development crowd, is that staff development as presently conducted does not work. More palatable, perhaps, is that its effects are the same for teachers of large and small classes.

The Effective Teacher Study in Project STAR

Under the direction and urging of Helen Bain, STAR researchers analyzed teachers and their teaching behaviors. Not all STAR data on teaching behaviors have yet been analyzed fully, but some results appear in the STAR report. Researchers interviewed teachers and aides at the end of each year to collect data on teacher concerns and ideas, grouping practices for instruction, use of volunteers, etc. Teachers and teacher aides kept logs of time use in the classrooms, responded to questionnaires about problems in classrooms, and provided personal and professional data, such as degrees earned, experience, etc.

To study effective and less effective teachers in Grades 2 and 3, researchers first ranked STAR classes as determined by class average test scores and by the largest standardized-test gain scores from one year to the next—a "value-added" idea. They selected 65 teachers from the top 10% (effective) and 60 from the lower 50% of teachers, based on those teachers' class-average gain scores on standardized tests. The two groups of teachers were very similar in terms of demographics and personal and professional qualifications, such as ethnicity, age, and preparation. Portions of those descriptive data are compared for the two groups in Table 5.1 (from Word et al., 1990, p. 41). All STAR teachers were certified to teach at their assigned grade levels. Most were on Level I of Tennessee's three-stage career ladder for teachers. There were, however, important differences in what happened in the classrooms of teachers in the two groups, according to results of observations and interviews. Besides important differences on the class-average test scores, statistically significant differences existed between effective and less effective teachers on several variables selected for analysis, including these:

1. Instruction is guided by a preplanned curriculum.
2. Students are carefully oriented to lessons.
3. Instruction is clear and focused.
4. Learning progress is monitored closely.
5. When students don't understand, they are retaught.
6. Class time is used for learning.
7. There are smooth, efficient routines.
8. Instructional groups formed in the classroom fit instructional needs.
9. Standards for behavior are explicit.
10. Personal interactions . . . are positive.
11. Rewards are used to promote excellence.

The only one of 12 criteria chosen for study that showed no difference between effective and less effective teachers was "high teacher expectations for student learning" (Table 5.2). This expression is almost as common today as "all students can learn" and may be more a politically correct comment than a driving force in classroom teaching behavior.

The researchers also observed important teaching practices and instructional strategies that most educators would agree are parts of effective teaching and learning in the classrooms of effective teachers. The researchers noted the following in classes of effective teachers (Word et al., 1990, pp. 259–262):

- Student participation in establishing classroom rules
- Excellent personal student interactions

TABLE 5.1 Professional and Personal Characteristics of Second- and Third-Grade Effective and Less Effective Teachers (from Word et al., p. 260). These two data categories denoted by the asterisk, however, are more than 10 percentage points different.

Characteristics	Effective (N = 65)	Less Effective (N = 60)
Race		
White	47 (72%)	48 (80%)
Black	18 (28%)	12 (20%)
Age		
29 and under	5 (8%)	11 (18%)
30–39	20 (31%)	20 (33%)
40–49	19 (29%)	19 (32%)
50–59	15 (23%)	6 (10%)
60 and above	6 (9%)	4 (7%)
Preparation		
B.A. or B.S.	38 (58%)	35 (58%)
M.A. or M.S.	27 (42%)	25 (42%)
Certification		
Full primary	65 (100%)	60 (100%)
Total years of teaching experience		
9 and under	16 (25%)	26 (43%)*
10 to 19	32 (49%)	26 (43%)
20 to 29	12 (19%)	3 (5%)*
30 and above	5 (8%)	5 (8%)
Career ladder level		
Not on career Ladder	5 (8%)	4 (7%)
Apprentice	3 (5%)	6 (10%)
Probationary	2 (3%)	5 (8%)
Level I	47 (72%)	40 (67%)
Level II	3 (4%)	3 (5%)
Level III	5 (8%)	2 (3%)

NOTE: The two groups are NOT significantly different in basic status or demographic data.

TABLE 5.2 Summary of Percentage Ratings on 12 Teaching Practices: Second- and Third-Grade Effective and Less Effective Teachers, Project STAR (adapted from Word et al., 1990, p. 261).

| | Teacher Ratings | | | |
| | Effective | | Less Effective | |
Criterion or Behavior	Lo (1, 2, 3)	Hi (4)	Lo (1, 2, 3)	Hi (4)
Instruction is guided by a preplanned curriculum.	17%	83%*	38%	62%
Expectations for student learning are high.	33%	67%	41%	59%
Students are carefully oriented to lessons.	23%	77%**	53%	48%
Instruction is clear and focused.	19%	81%***	59%	41%
Learning progress is monitored closely.	19%	81%***	51%	49%
When students don't understand, they are retaught.	22%	78%*	45%	55%
Class time is used for learning.	13%	87%***	48%	52%
There are smooth, efficient classroom routines.	11%	89%***	45%	55%
Instructional groups formed in the classroom fit instructional needs.	19%	81%*	38%	62%
Standards for classroom behavior are explicit.	14%	86%***	44%	56%
Personal interactions between teacher and students are positive.	13%	88%***	44%	56%
Incentives and rewards for students are used to promote excellence.	18%	82%*	37%	63%

$*p < .05$, $**p < .01$, $***p < .001$. Percents are rounded.

- Learning centers
- Parent volunteers
- Manipulatives in math
- Field trips
- Peer tutoring

This portion of STAR was a study of effective and less effective teachers based upon gain scores of students, and *not specifically a study of teachers in small and large classes*. Yet, as Word et al., 1990, p. 37, reported, in Grades 2 and 3, 68% and 78%, respectively, of the top 10% of STAR classes as determined by gain scores were S classes. It stands to reason that most of the "most effective" teachers in this analysis were in STAR S classes, but with approximately 35% of all classes being S, the S classes were greatly overrepresented in the top-scoring classes category. If so, then most of the less effective teachers were in R and RA classes, a strange finding given the random assignment and the similar demographics shown in Table 5.1. Because of their greater success, those teaching practices observed in classrooms of the effective teachers might be themes for staff development. Yet, the question would remain, Did all STAR teachers know these things, but some were hindered by class size from doing them?

Because this aspect of STAR was observational and not experimental, researchers could only speculate if the teaching practices produced the positive outcomes or if the positive outcomes influenced teachers to teach better. Teaching and learning—and also student and teacher morale—are reciprocal. Through observation, analysis of questionnaire responses, and logs of time use, etc. we may learn how more effective teachers take advantage of a small class to improve student outcomes. Effective teachers established a positive environment for student learning, growth, and development in Project STAR, regardless of the class size, but something was different—class size.

Teacher Behavior Derived From Analysis of Interviews

Johnston (1990) summarized the results of teacher interviews that researchers conducted at the end of each year of STAR. The nearly 1,100 interviews covered a range of questions and issues, but the key focus was on what differences teachers perceived from their teaching

TABLE 5.3 Numbers of Interviews Conducted With Project STAR Teachers in May of Each Teaching Year 1986–1989

| | Numbers of May Interviews by Year, Grade, and Class Type | | | | |
Class Type	1986 (K)	1987 (1)	1988 (2)	1989 (3)	Totals (K–3)
Small (S)	128	126	86	88	428
Regular (R)	101	113	54	55	323
Regular/aide (RA)	99	107	71	70	347
Totals	328	346	211	213	1098

in the three class types in STAR: S, R, and RA. Table 5.3 shows the distribution by year and class type of the interviews with STAR teachers. There were fewer interviews in Grades 2 and 3 because some teachers participated in the Grade-2 training study, and because answers in Grades 2 and 3 were consistent with results obtained in K and Grade-1 interviews, so there was little value in continuing to interview all teachers. The many interviews across all four years of STAR provided a clear picture of how teachers perceived teaching conditions in the different class types.

Researchers followed careful procedures and content analysis steps to identify common themes and categories in the responses. The iterative process produced 17 categories, of which 14 related specifically to teachers' perceptions of teaching in either a S, R, or RA classroom (Johnston, 1990, p. 104). The 14 categories of teacher responses displayed in Table 5.4 were the basis for analyzing teaching behaviors (Johnston, 1990, pp. 4–6).

Slight modifications were made in the interview protocols during the third year of STAR (second grade). The new questions requested that teachers address directly any perceived differences in some of the categories in Table 5.4 when the class sizes changed. According to Johnston (1990, p. 5), "The broad purpose of these exit interviews was to identify and describe those aspects of classroom teaching that teachers experienced differently in comparison to the previous year's experience in a regular size class."

The differences in teaching between and among the class types could be approached two ways. Teachers could compare the present

TABLE 5.4 The 14 Categories of Teaching Behavior Derived From Interviews With STAR Teachers (1986–1989) and Used to Analyze Teaching in Varying-Sized Classes

- Grouping of students
- Physical environment
- Learning centers
- Social climate
    Interactions
    Cooperation
    Teacher knowledge of
    student
- Enrichment activities
- Classroom management
    Problem behaviors
    Dealing with disruptions
- Monitor/evaluate progress
- Planning and preparation
- Individual attention to students

- Morale
    Satisfaction
    Stress
    Frustration
    Attitude toward work
- Amount and rate of pupil progress
- Parent–teacher relations
- Teachers aides
    Yes/no
    Quality
    Duties
- Instruction
    - Methods and techniques
    - Curriculum
    - Goals

year with the past year, but teachers with regular classes both years would have few differences to discuss. However, for each year some teachers represented all three class types (S, R, RA). The overall picture from teacher interviews revealed that teacher perceptions of the 14 categories differed between small and regular classes (S vs. R) and between regular-aide classes and regular classes (RA vs. R). Perceptions of S and RA teachers were quite similar. The result was that teacher perceptions were clustered into R vs. S + RA. According to Johnston (1990, p. 6), "With very few exceptions, differences reported by K–3 S and RA teachers were essentially similar." Differences were consistent across grades (K–3).

One dimension in STAR interviews referred to the "quality of the teacher's work life." Teaching is hard work. Teachers extend their work into their personal lives in many ways: planning, correcting student work, attending school functions, maintaining or improving their skills through staff development, even selecting and buying supplies and materials for the classroom, often using their own resources. Smaller classes can influence at least one dimension of the outside-of-class work, correcting student papers and work. Johnston (1990) summarized the interview responses about the quality of the teacher's work life; some of Johnston's summary is reproduced here because it seems important and few other studies have emphasized quality of work in such detail. (Abbreviations for class size [S, R, and RA] were not in the original text.)

Quality of Work Life (Johnston, 1990)

The S and RA teachers reported that they felt more relaxed, less pressured, and more satisfied at the end of the day. Time appeared to be an important factor in these teachers' perceptions of their work life. They felt less pressured because they knew they would be able to get the required basic instruction completed. They felt more satisfied because they were able to interact more frequently with each child on both a personal and academic level. They felt satisfied because they did not have to be as controlling and because they had the time to be more flexible in meeting individual pupil needs using more developmentally appropriate approaches. Their satisfaction extended to their home life, with many K–3 S and RA teachers reporting that they did not take as much work home as they had when teaching a R class. In sum, S and RA teachers felt that they were able to accomplish more using more desirable methods than they could when teaching in a R class (Johnston, 1990, pp. 14–15).

Researchers analyzed the teachers' interview responses to all 14 categories and summarized them in a manner similar to responses in the quality-of-work-life category. Johnston (1990) presented these results cogently and clearly. Johnston's summary of four years of teacher interviews is a qualitative picture of differences in the class conditions. In reading this summary, recall that the regular (R) class teachers in STAR had classes of only about 25 students, some fewer than the numbers of students many teachers face each day. Krueger (1997) demonstrated that quantitative differences *within* the STAR R classes—the control group—showed the class-size effect. The achievement of the smaller R classes (about 22 students) was greater than the achievement of the larger R classes. It seems very likely that the positive perceptions of S and RA teachers about teaching in elementary classes in the late 1980s when compared to responses of R teachers who had classes smaller than the classes of many teachers today provide a true, and somewhat conservative, picture. Teachers of R classes make up one group, and the combined responses of S and RA teachers constitute the second group.

Here, with minor editing, is Johnston's (1990, pp. 15-16) summary of the interviews.

Conclusions From Project STAR Teacher Interviews

The following differences are apparent between instruction in S and RA classes, and instruction in R classes. Basic instruction is completed more quickly providing more available time. Small and RA teachers used this newly available time for covering additional basic material, use of supplemental text and enrichment activities, more in-depth instruction regarding the basic content, more frequent opportunities for children to engage in first-hand learning activities using concrete materials, and increased use of learning centers. These patterns emerged in K and continued through the third grade.

Improved ability to individualize instruction emerged as a dominant theme in S and RA teachers' perceptions of differences between instruction in S and RA classes and R classes. Again citing extra available time as the crucial factor, S and RA teachers reported increased monitoring of pupil behavior and learning, opportunities for more immediate and more individualized reteaching or enrichment, more frequent interactions with each child, and a better match between each child's ability and the instructional opportunities provided. Small and RA teachers perceived that they had a more detailed and accessible knowledge of each child's needs as a learner. Moreover, they felt that they had more time available to meet individual learner's needs using a variety of instructional approaches. Small class size or the presence of a full-time teacher's aide fostered the increased use of learning approaches generally considered by educators to be highly desirable, developmentally appropriate primary-grade practices.

Significant reduction of class size, or the addition of a full-time aide, also makes positive changes in the physical, social, and emotional environments in primary-grade classrooms. Classrooms are more humane and pleasant work environments for both teachers and children. Teachers and children are under less stress and learning occurs in a more relaxed atmosphere. Children are less likely to get lost in the crowd, and are more likely to have their own unique needs met by adults who have a better understanding of them as individuals. The extent to which teachers, aides, and children are friendly, supportive, and trusting of one another is an indication of the peer cohesion of children and the esprit de corps of the group as a whole (Johnston & Davis, 1989, pp. 15-16). This dimension is an indicator of classroom morale and sense of team spirit, and is known to be characteristic of effective elementary schools.

This careful and concise summary of over 1,000 interviews is anecdotal evidence of differences in class-size conditions and effects as perceived by teachers who experienced them in the same building with randomly assigned students. Add these qualitative comments to the details in Chapter 4, especially to the Project Success and SSS information for recent studies, and to the Lindbloom (1970), Olson (1971), Filby et al. (1980), and Cooper (1989a) summaries for older class-size studies, and the picture becomes very clear. It is a picture of the elementary-school experiences that many adults refer to as "the good old days." Why do adults hesitate to offer these experiences to young children today?

A challenge is to translate the information provided in these interviews into useful staff development sessions for teachers of 15:1 classes. Do these interview results help staff development persons know what to teach to teachers of 15:1 classes? How might persons evaluate such staff development efforts and then determine if any change in student outcomes would be related to staff development or to the change in class sizes?

6

Small Classes
Provide Benefits
for Students

We need to consider a broad range of outcomes—the relationship between class size and the quality and humanness of the nation's schools.

(Cahen & Filby, 1979, p. 538)

Class size affects the quality of the classroom environment.

(Smith & Glass, 1979, p. 46)

Educators have long argued that those who "evaluate" or critique education outcomes should take a broad and long-range view of student achievement. Yet, most education critics and policy persons seek immediate benefits usually narrowly expressed as standardized test scores and comparisons among groups based on standardized or norm-referenced tests (NRT). A long-range and wide-angle view seems more realistic than to consider test scores only, but results in this chapter rely heavily upon test-score comparisons that are supported by other indicators.

It is difficult to draw an absolute line between how a student benefits from small classes and how small classes benefit others, such as teachers, parents, or society as a whole. For example, if students learn more or behave better in classes, teachers may sense increases in their own efficacy, morale, energy, etc. Parents may report that students are more involved in schooling or that they behave better at home. Nevertheless, the *major* emphasis in this chapter is on small-class benefits as demonstrated by *student* outcomes.

It may also be difficult to attribute student achievement gains only to small classes. Seldom is there just a single change in an education program. For example, when class size is changed, individual teachers may adopt new programs or approaches to teaching. If a program is adopted districtwide, separating the effects of each program or attributing a portion of the observed gains to one program or another can be problematic. For example, Success for All (SFA) is a popular remediation program that relies, among other things, on small classes and on tutoring (very small classes) to obtain its gains. What proportion of SFA gains can be attributed *only* to the small-class effect? The same question could be asked about any program that gets extra gains *and* employs small classes as part of its design. Another scenario: When the Clovis Unified School District (CUSD) in Clovis, California, began to participate in the California Class-Size Reduction (CSR) effort, district leaders also initiated the Early Literacy Program.

The CUSD Division of Assessment undertook the task of understanding student gains in Grade 1 by comparing results from before and after beginning CSR and Early Literacy. Evaluators used several measures of reading achievement that both CSR and the Early Literacy effort could influence. The gains obtained on running records seemed impressive, but in examining the pilot results, how can policy persons determine what part of the gain might legitimately be from CSR and what part might be from Early Literacy? Table 6.1 shows the pilot results as provided by the CUSD Division of Assessment (draft, 10/98). Remember that correlation is not cause.

The Degrees of Reading Power (DRP) test was administered to first-grade students in the spring of 1997 and 1998. The percentage of students scoring at or above the 50th percentile on the DRP is indicated in Table 6.1. Table 6.1 also shows CUSD's 50th percentile

TABLE 6.1 Comparison of Grade-1 Degrees of Reading Power (DRP) Test Scores in 1997 and 1998 After Class-Size Reduction (CSR) and Use of Early Literacy in One California School System

Degrees of Reading Power	1997	1998	Gain
CUSD 50th percentile score	15	21	+6
National 50th percentile score	15	15	NA
Percentage at/above 50th percentile	50.2	68.1	+17.9%

DRP score compared to the national 50th percentile DRP score for spring 1997 and spring 1998.

Because these test results reflect at least two "treatments," CSR and Early Literacy, and because there is no appropriate control group—although the national percentile is a benchmark—the scores themselves do not allow a conclusion that CSR caused the change. The scores do not show what part of the gain might be connected to CSR or to Early Literacy, or to the unique blend of the two treatments in this particular district. More time and added analyses will be needed to sort out possible effects of CSR in these impressive gains at Grade 1. Results at CUSD are not unlike results obtained in other carefully controlled studies of class size. Thus, comparisons of CUSD results to external class-size studies may provide added benchmarks and a sense of consistency through simultaneous replication.

What other steps might be taken to separate the class size-effect from, for example, the Early Literacy initiative? Because Early Literacy is directly related to reading outcomes, and because class size and CSR should influence all tests, an analysis of math gains (if the tests are available) might provide added indications of the CSR influence. One advantage of CSR is that it is administratively mutable and easy to determine if the change has been implemented—simply *count* the youngsters in the classroom. In a complex treatment such as Early Literacy, the fidelity of the innovation and the degree of the implementation must be known before inferences can be drawn about the impact of the treatment on outcomes. Simply said, you should not attribute gains to a treatment until you have evaluated if and how the treatment was implemented.

The Fairfax County, Virginia Public Schools (FCPS) instituted a "Reduced-Ratio Program" specifically "to provide support for aca-

TABLE 6.2 Percentage of Program and Nonprogram FCPS
Grade-2 Students (S) Passing the Running Record Test by SES[a]

	Free/Reduced Meals ($n = 158$)	Non-Free/Reduced Meals ($n = 170$)	Mean % Difference
Program students, $n = 233$	75%	89%	14%
Nonprogram students $n = 95$	54%	84%	30%
Mean % difference	21%	5%	16%

[a] Adapted from Fairfax County (1997, p. 23, Table 8).

demically at-risk first grade students" (Fairfax County, 1997, p. ES-1).
Following the research outcomes of earlier class-size reviews and
studies, the FCPS instituted the program by reducing class sizes from
an average of 22 to 15 in first grades in schools with high densities
of at-risk students. Schools were phased-in with 15 in January 1992;
16 in September 1992, and 17 later "for a total of 48 reduced-ratio
schools" (Fairfax County, 1997, p. ES-1). Staff development to improve math and reading instruction was provided and evaluated to
see that teachers used the preferred techniques in their classrooms.
The report does not specify if all or only reduced-ratio first-grade
teachers received this instruction.

Although the FCPS effort is not an experiment, researchers used
several comparisons to strengthen the analyses of this small-class
effort to "improve the academic achievement of at-risk students"
(Fairfax County, 1997, p. ES-2). Schools with higher densities of at-
risk students were in the study, (program students), so comparisons
were possible with other sites (nonprogram students). The stag-
gered starts provided cohort analyses over time. The FCPS small
classes were in Grade 1, but the data in Table 6.2 show Grade-2
comparisons for program and nonprogram students by free and
reduced-price meals used as a surrogate for socioeconomic status
(SES).

Data in Table 6.2 show the powerful difference in performance
on Grade-2 criterion-referenced tests of low-SES students depending

upon their class size in Grade 1: 21% more low-SES program students (75%) passed the test than did nonprogram low-SES students (54%) one year after the small-class "treatment." Nonprogram low-SES students had a 54% passing rate compared to an 84% passing rate for nonprogram and higher-SES students, or an achievement-gap difference of 30%. When the low-SES students' passing rate of 75% is compared to the nonprogram and higher-SES students' passing rate of 84%, the achievement-gap difference is only 9%. Once again this shows (a) the influence of SES on the "difficulty of the educational task" (Cooley, 1993) and (b) the influence of small classes to close this achievement gap between SES levels on criterion-referenced tests.

The 17.9% gain in Table 6.1 and the 21% gain in Table 6.2 are similar to the 17.3% gain found in STAR on the criterion-referenced test results in Grade 1 (Finn & Achilles, 1990, p. 593). The similarity found in single-district studies gives "real-life credibility" to results found in large-scale experiments.

Why do some people continue to say that "class size doesn't matter" when the data over many years, teacher reports, and common sense overwhelmingly support small classes for little kids? Although class-size studies conducted prior to 1984 or so provided mixed results about class size and student achievement, the Glass and Smith (1978) and the Smith and Glass (1979) meta-analyses showed that class size brought about many positive student (and other) benefits. The Glass and Smith (1978) meta-analysis offered clues for the lack of consistent class-size and achievement results. Analyses of STAR data provided explanations for some inconsistent results of early class-size studies that used easily measured student outcomes as the criterion variables.

Cahen and Filby (1979) commented that over half of the 725 Glass and Smith comparisons and indicators of class-size effects came from studies conducted before 1940. When analyzing their class-size studies, Glass and Smith (1978, p. 493) found ". . . no correlation between class size and achievement advantage in the studies conducted before 1940." Before 1940, some studies were designed around achievement differences in classes of 40 and 35, or 35 and 30, *where the classes of 35 or of 30 were defined as small.* The research was not sensitive to differences in achievement between classes of these sizes—if there were, in fact, consistent differences. The PTR was seldom noted, nor were differences in teacher preparation.

Glass and Smith found consistent differences between the achievement advantages of students in small classes over those in large classes in well-designed and controlled studies when compared to results in poorly designed and controlled studies. The better the study, the more likely that there were differences in outcomes between large and small classes and that the differences were detected. Cahen and Filby (1979, p. 493) said of this aspect of the Glass and Smith analysis, "The overall difference in results between the well-controlled and the poorly controlled studies was dramatic. The curve for the poorly designed studies was almost flat, indicating, at best, a very small advantage to smaller classes." Because nearly half of the Glass and Smith indicators of class-size effects in the studies conducted between about 1900 and 1976 came from weak studies, Cahen and Filby (1979, p. 493) were able to conclude, "Little wonder class-size research has been so inconclusive."

Two reasons that class size and student achievement connections have not seemed conclusive or consistent in the early research are that the early studies may not have been well controlled, designed, or conducted, and they may have focused on class sizes that were too large to provide positive and consistent results (i.e., classes larger than 30 or 35 students). Researchers today have been able to learn much from the early class-size studies.

Project STAR's longitudinal nature, small classes starting in kindergarten (K), use of the second experimental condition of the full-time teacher aide, and other careful design elements helped sort out some of the confusion over the early class size and achievement results. STAR, including the LBS and Challenge, showed that students did better if they *began* their educational experiences in small classes, that is, in Grades K or 1. STAR showed that the use of another adult, in this case a full-time instructional aide, in a regular-sized class of about 25 students (25:1 plus an aide) did *not* generally have a positive short-term effect on student achievement.

Bain et al. (1997) reviewed the long-term effects associated with small-class intervention in early primary grades. Their study showed that benefits were stronger for students who had more than one year of small classes, that benefits were long-term, and that benefits were not just academic test results. Small-class students were more likely than large-class students to participate in school and identify with schooling (e.g., Finn, 1993, 1998; Finn & Cox, 1992). Students who started school in small classes were more likely to have higher high school grades and take more difficult classes like calculus and foreign languages, and to be in trouble in school (truant, suspended) or be retained in grade *less often* than their peers who were in larger classes in primary grades (Bain et al., 1997). Some other reasons that early studies of class size and student achievement connections did not seem conclusive emerged from analyses of the STAR results:

- Early studies may have been too brief in duration to show consistently positive results or to show long-term outcomes.
- Early studies, especially large-scale studies, may have used a second adult in a large class as a way to "reduce" class size.
- Researchers may have considered PTR and class size as synonyms.
- Early studies may have defined student achievement too narrowly, confining achievement only to academics as measured easily by group tests.

Well-designed class-size studies have consistently documented a class-size effect. Academic achievement increases when class sizes get smaller (below 20), and academic achievement rises rapidly as class sizes reduce between 15:1 and one-on-one tutoring. Yet academics, or test scores, constitute only one indication of positive student achievement outcomes. Improved student outcomes in small classes occur in at least four general areas that, for ease of discussion, are categorized as A, B, C, and D, and are called the *Abecedarian Covenant.* Here are brief descriptions of ABCD outcomes:

Academics are such indicators of achievement as higher test scores, and selection and completion of advanced courses—advanced placement, calculus, foreign languages.

Behavior in school is improved when there are fewer discipline referrals, greater time-on-task, and better student deportment including elements of participation such as turning in homework and engagement in class activities.

Citizenship is indicated by positive presence in school and society. Students may accept leadership roles and participate in school-sanctioned events (clubs, government).

TABLE 6.3 Selected Demographic Indicators for Burke County, NC Schools, 1992–1998

	1992–1993		1997–1998		Change		
Indicator	n	%	n	%	n	%[a]	%[b]
District							
enrollment	12,400	100	13,765	100	+1365	—	11
Free-lunch							
eligible	3,583	29	5,199	38	+1616	+9	45
Limited English							
proficient							
(LEP)	217	1.8	1,135	8.2	+918	+6.4	423

[a] Percentage difference, not percent change.

[b] Percent change (1993–1998).

> *Development* is a general human growth category indicated by such things as post-high-school plans and maturing behaviors. Other productive out-of-school behaviors, such as helpfulness, volunteering, and fewer arrests, are signs of student development.

The first category of student benefits from small classes is achievement comparisons on tests of academics. Here are some recent results from well-designed class-size efforts.

Academics: Burke County, North Carolina

In addition to the effect–size analyses of test-score differences (Achilles, Harman, & Egelson, 1995), Burke County teachers and administrators have been tracking student outcomes and test-score results on the End-of-Grade (EOG) tests given in North Carolina in Grade 3. Burke County began phasing in small classes in a pilot-study manner and by 1996–1997 all students in Grades 1–3 had experienced small (17:1 or so) classes if they had been in the system for those grades. Burke County had demographic indicators, 1992–1993 through 1997–1998, that in many districts would presage declining test scores (see Table 6.3).

TABLE 6.4 Reading Proficiency Levels on Grade-3 End-of-Grade Tests, 1993–1998, Burke County, NC, for Reading and Math (*n* and %)

Test Year and Subject	N	Level 1		Level 4		Levels 3 & 4	
		n	%	*n*	%	*n*	%
Reading							
1993	951	127	13.4	192	20.2	573	60.3
1998	1103	48	4.4	455	41.3	880	79.8
% Diff.	NA	NA	−9.0	NA	+21.1	NA	+19.5
Math							
1993	951	104	10.9	187	19.7	586	61.6
1998	1103	26	2.4	305	27.7	838	76.0
% Diff.	NA	NA	−8.5	NA	+8.0	NA	+14.4

The demographic-driven challenges for Burke County education are evident in Table 6.3 data: Although district total enrollment increased about 11%, the percentage of free-lunch (45%) and LEP students (423%) increased far more rapidly than did the enrollment. Such data suggest that educators would need to make massive efforts to keep achievement indicators from falling. Rather than falling, achievement levels on reading and math on the Grade-3 EOG tests have increased as small classes in Grades 1–3 have become available to all students. On EOG tests, proficiency level 1 is lowest, an unacceptable level of performance. Levels 3 and 4 are proficient, with level 4 highly acceptable. Data in Table 6.4 show the impact and growth of the "small-class effect" in Burke County.

As class sizes have been reduced, Burke County has moved up from ranking 43rd of 117 North Carolina school districts to ranking 13th of 117 districts in 1998. The county has achieved this in spite of the disproportionate growth of free-lunch and LEP students, and its generally weak tax base—it is one of a few North Carolina districts that qualify for special low-wealth assistance from the state.

Although the gains in levels 3 and 4 are impressive—from 60.3% to 79.8% at proficiency in reading and 61.6% to 76% in math, the decline in the lowest levels of proficiency is most satisfying, from 13.4% to 4.4% at level 1 in reading and from 10.9% to 2.4% in math. To relieve the poorest-performing students of their burden of low proficiency in the face of the increasing difficulty of achieving this educational goal as measured by demographic indicators is truly gratifying. These results are believable and consistent with findings in other class-size research that the hard-to-teach students get greater benefits from small classes than do average or better students (e.g., Finn & Achilles, 1990; Robinson, 1990; Wenglinsky, 1997).

The hard-to-teach students get greater benefits from small classes than do average or better students.

Cumulative Student Academic Benefits

Besides cross-sectional (one-year) reviews of student academic differences in smaller and larger classes, such as the Grade-3 analyses in Burke County, researchers can also look for longitudinal or cumulative differences in student academic benefits from small classes. This requires the researchers to track *students* by class types for several years, a time-consuming and difficult task. A second way to infer cumulative benefits is to track student test-score *outcome trends* by class types over several years. For example, if small classes S in STAR were 40% of all classes in the first year (kindergarten), we might expect that about 40% of the top 10% of STAR classes on standardized achievement test scores would be S. As shown in Table 6.5, this is not the case.

In K, S classes were 40% of all STAR classes, but 55% of the top 10% of classes on the standardized test. This is 15% more than might be expected. The percentage difference between the percentage of STAR S classes in a given grade level and the percent of S classes scoring in the top 10% of all classes on a standardized test increases over time from K to Grade 3: 15, 28, 29, 37. By Grade 3, although S classes are 41% of all STAR classes, the S classes are 78% of the top-scoring classes, or nearly twice what would be expected by proportion alone. In a proportionate manner, the relative percentage of regular R and regular-with-aide RA classes in the top 10% of classes on the standardized test scores declines each year as shown by the negative numbers in Table 6.5.

TABLE 6.5 Cumulative Effects of Small Classes From Project STAR: Top 10% of Classes, K–3, STAR on SAT, Reading[a]

| | Top 10% of Classes, K–3 by Class Types (S, R, RA) in STAR | | | | | | | | | | | | |
| | Small (S) | | | | Regular (R) | | | | Reg. Aide (RA) | | | | Total | |
Grade	n	%	% of N[b]	Diff %	n	%	% of N[b]	Diff %	n	%	% of N[b]	Diff %	N	%
K	18	55	40	+15	10	30	30	0	5	15	30	−15	33	100
1	22	65	37	+28	5	15	34	−19	7	21	29	−8	34	101[c]
2	23	68	39	+29	5	15	29	−14	6	18	32	−14	34	101[c]
3	25	78	41	+37	2	6	27	−27	5	16	32	−16	32	100

[a] Word et al. (1990, p. 37, Table III-13). Percents have been computed and added to make interpretation easier. Adaptations include abbreviations. All percents rounded.

[b] Percent of total classes (N) each year of each type (see Word et al., 1990, Table A-1; see Appendix A for N).

[c] Rounding caused deviation from 100%.

TABLE 6.6 Academic Benefits of Small (1:15–1:20) Classes Summarized from Selected Studies

Source/Subject[a]	Effect Size (ES) or Difference: Small Class Advantage				Notes or Comments
1. Glass & Smith (1978)[a]	.40 (well-designed studies)				No differences between reading & math reported in Cahen & Filby (1979, p. 493)
2. STAR (by grades)					
a. Original	K .21	1st .34	2nd .26	3rd .24	Range .13 to .40 with added benefit to minority (Finn & Achilles, 1998)
b. Reanalysis[b]	.52	.45	.63	.63	Comparing classes of 13–15 vs. 23–27 (Boyd-Zaharias et al., 1995)
c. Class-level[b] 1	—	.64			Finn & Achilles (1990, p. 566)
2	—	—	17% gain for minority students		Finn & Achilles (1990, p. 566)
d. LBS (by grades)	4th .13	5th .22	6th .21	7th .15	Reported in Finn & Achilles (1998) as taken from various LBS reports
3. SAGE (Molnar, 1998)	12% test-score advantage for small classes, on average, over large classes in Grade 1				

TABLE 6.6 (Continued)

Source/Subject[a]	Effect Size (ES) or Difference: Small Class Advantage	Notes or Comments
4. Burke Co., NC, Grade 3	a. .37 ES for students matched as second graders b. .56 ES for students matched as first graders c. .65 ES for End-of-Grade tests, Grade 3	Achilles, Harman, and Egelson (1995) Burke Co. Public Schools (1998)
5. Fairfax Co. VA	21% greater passing rate for low SES students, Grade 2	Fairfax County (1997)
6. Clovis, CA (1998)	17.9% increase in grade-1 reading	CUSD Office of Assessment (1998)

[a] Data are for reading scores. Glass and Smith reported no difference in benefits between reading and math. STAR and LBS results between reading and math were similar. Burke Co. math was slightly better than reading. SAGE results were similar for reading and for math. Class size benefits for reading and math are consistently about the same magnitude.

[b] In one reanalysis, .56, the average reading ES for STAR, is similar to the ES by classes presented by Finn and Achilles. Class-level ES is not usually estimated, but STAR was a study of class size. The Glass and Smith estimate of .40 is about mid-point of STAR original analysis which included the "out-of-range" classes (see Appendix A), and the reanalysis which corrected for "out-of-range" classes.

Academic Achievement Benefits From Other Studies

Student academic achievement benefits favoring students in smaller rather than larger classes have been found in all recent well-designed and -conducted class-size studies. These studies include Wisconsin's Student Achievement Guarantee in Education (SAGE) effort; Burke County, NC; Success Starts Small (SSS); and the Lasting Benefits Study (LBS) that followed STAR students in Grades 4–8. Table 6.6 summarizes academic achievement differences obtained in recent studies, often reported in effect size, or ES. An ES of 0.3 is usually considered educationally significant or important. (For a clear discussion of ES, see Mosteller, 1995, p. 120).

Finn and Achilles (1990, p. 566) estimated a class-level effect size in reading for STAR S classes at Grade 1 as 0.64. The ES is not usually calculated for classes, so there is little base of comparison for this ES, except in the reanalysis that researchers did for classes of 13–15 vs. classes of 23–27 (Boyd-Zaharias, Achilles, Nye, & Fulton, 1995) that produced ESs of 0.52, 0.45, 0.63, and 0.63 for Grades K through 3, respectively. STAR data are being re-analyzed and ES computations are being reviewed (Finn & Achilles, 1998).

Unlike statistical significance, ES is not influenced by sample size. The ES explains how much a person who scores at the mean, or 50th percentile, would move up the "normal" distribution in terms of standard deviation units. A person who scored about the 50th percentile before a treatment would score about the 69th percentile if the treatment had an ES of 0.5. The positive, educationally important academic achievement benefits of S classes are consistent in all studies reported on Table 6.6. The consistency and similarity of the results provide one source of confidence in the "small-class" effect.

A Student Equity Factor

Many class-size researchers have described differential benefits that accrue to different groups of students from being in S. Males and females consistently benefit equally from being in S. Student benefits are greater for low-SES, minority, and hard-to-teach students than for average or above-average students (Boozer & Rouse, 1995; Finn & Achilles, 1990; Robinson, 1990; Wenglinsky, 1997).

TABLE 6.7 Small-Class Advantage, Grade 1, STAR, by Race, on Criterion-Referenced (BSF) Tests (% Correct) and on the Normed Stanford Achievement Test (Score Differences)[a]

Test	White Ave. Diff. S vs. Other	Minority Ave. Diff. S vs. Other	Small-Class Advantage[b] Minority Over White
SAT Read.[c]	8.6	16.7	+8.1 points
SAT Math	9.0	11.6	+2.6 points
BSF Read.[c]	4.8%	17.3%	+12.5%
BSF Math	3.1%	7.0%	+3.9%

[a] Adapted from Finn and Achilles (1990, p. 567).

[b] Advantage is computed by S score minus R plus RA score divided by two, or S vs. all others.

[c] SAT is test-score difference; BSF is difference in percentage of items correct.

Table 6.7 shows the small-class advantage for Grade-1 minority students in STAR (Finn & Achilles, 1990). The minority-benefit difference was for all STAR Grade-1 students on both standardized and on criterion-referenced Basic Skill First (BSF) tests. Comparisons are S vs. both other STAR conditions, R and RA. *Minority students get at least double the benefits as nonminority students from S classes* (work still in progress).

Table 6.8 shows the Grade-1 white-minority difference on the percentage of correct responses on the criterion-referenced BSF test among all three STAR class types (S, R, RA) analyzed by when a student began the STAR experience, either in K or Grade 1. There are two clear achievement differences: (1) Small-class students do better than students in the other two class types (R and RA), and (2) students who enter school in K do better on Grade-1 tests than do students who enter school in Grade 1 (hey, they have one more year of school!) On average, a minority student who enters K in S gets about the same percentage of correct answers on the BSF test as does the nonminority student. This result raises a troublesome problem. Is it possible that present schooling practices of no full-day K or of large-class K conditions actually *contribute* to the achievement gap that educators and federal education programs such as Title I try to eliminate or reduce by spending billions of dollars and thousands of difficult hours? More research is needed to explore these directions.

TABLE 6.8 Percent of Criterion-Referenced Test (BSF) Items Correct, Grade 1, STAR, by Race (White/Minority), by Class Type (S, R, RA), and by Time of Entry (K or 1).[a]

Class Type & Student	Grade of Entry to STAR[b]		Ave. % Diff. (K Advantage)
	Enter in K % Correct	Enter in 1 % Correct	
Small			
White	88	85	+3
Minority	88	79	+9
Regular (reg)			
White	86	80	+6
Minority	77	74	+3
Reg/Aide			
White	86	82	+4
Minority	79	77	+2
Small vs. regular: small-class advantage (%)			
White	+2	+5	NA
Minority	+11	+5	NA

[a] Adapted from Achilles, Nye, and Bain (1994-1995, p. 8).

[b] All percentages rounded.

Retention-in-Grade "Nonbenefit"

Why is a reduction in retention in grade a student benefit? Research over many years has demonstrated the inefficacy of this commonly used education practice. Yet, the practice continues to be employed and may even increase as leaders require higher "standards" but provide no extra funds for remediation. As the brief discussion of retention presented here shows, a reduction in grade retention is a positive outcome for students. Holmes and Matthews (1984) found negative effects of nonpromotion on elementary and junior high students, and Holmes (1989) substantiated the earlier findings. Reynolds (1992, p. 101) studied grade retention and concluded, "The findings of this study do not support grade retention as an educational practice." Pediatricians have studied grade retention and found that "both old-for-grade status and grade retention are independently associated with increased rates of behavior problems" (Byrd, Weitzman, & Auinger, 1997, p. 654).

TABLE 6.9 Range of Average Scores for Promotion or Retention in Grade, STAR, Kindergarten to Grade 1, SESAT TEST[a]

| | Average Score by Class Placement | | |
Decision	Small	Reg	Reg/Aide
Promote	441	435	436
Retain	422[b]	427[b]	421
Difference	19	8	15

[a] Adapted from Boyd-Zaharias et al. (1995, p. 117).

[b] On average, a student scoring 422, 423, 424, 425, or 426 would be promoted in a small class, but retained in a larger class in these comparisons.

Discussion of not retaining pupils in grade may lead to near-hysterical polarizations ("Either you favor social promotion and re-warding kids for failure, or you will retain them until they perform up to standards"). What is as inane as *only* these two options when research consistently shows that one doesn't work? There are many practices *other than* these two options: small classes, nongraded, peer tutoring, extended day, year-around schooling, etc. "But these steps are expensive," one might say. Perhaps, but if schooling costs $5,000/year per pupil and J. Doe spends 2 years in Grade 1, the costs is $10,000 for Grade 1 for J. Doe, *and retention does not work*. How might educators better spend some of the now-wasted extra $5,000? What are the true costs of alternatives? "U. S. school districts spend nearly $10 billion a year to pay for the extra year of schooling necessitated by retaining 2.4 million students" (Shepard & Smith, 1990, p. 88). This was almost 10 years *before* the retention craze driven by "higher standards." Using STAR data, Harvey (1993, 1994) reviewed both the negative outcomes of retention in grade and the positive reduction in grade retention found in small classes. Table 6.9 data demonstrate part of the class-size and retention-in-grade connection. Note that the average score for promoted students in STAR S classes was 441. The average score for promoted students in R classes was 435 and in RA classes the score was 436. Those differences are not surprises, given that students in S classes consistently outscored students in both the other class conditions.

The average scores for retaining a student in grade, however, between S and RA classes and the R classes (i.e., a class with one teacher and about 25 students) were a clear indicator of the S advantage. If our hypothetical student, Pat, were in an S class and received a score of 422, 423, 424, 425, or 426, Pat would have been promoted. *With those same scores in the R class, Pat would have been retained in K: Pat could have failed K based only on class size.*

In STAR, students remained in their assigned class types (S, R, RA) for Grades K–3. Apparently if the K teacher knew that Pat would be in an S first-grade class, or that Pat's first-grade teacher would have the help of an aide, the K teacher was willing to promote Pat with a lower score than if Pat would be in a R class. The cumulative outperformance of S vs. R classes in STAR presented in Table 6.9 shows little or no evidence of a penalty to later class-average scores of promoting students with scores of 422–426 in S classes. There also is *no* benefit to class average scores in later R classes from keeping low-scoring students from advancing with their peers.

A second inference from the scores in Table 6.9 is that in S and in RA classes teachers seemed to believe that they can succeed with a wider range of student abilities (19 score points) than in R classes (8 score points). In the typical large class, teachers may try to *reduce* the range of student abilities that they must work with by employing retention.

Special-Education Identification in Kindergarten

If a student needs special-education services, the sooner that student is identified and can receive services, the better. If the need is caught immediately, the problem may be remediated and the student may not need years of expensive special-education treatment. A student who needs services but whose problem is not identified may not improve and may spend many years in expensive special-education placements. Data in Table 6.10 show how S placement increases the probability that a student will be identified as needing early special-education help and how placement in (R) and especially in (RA) will reduce the probability that a student's special behavior or learning needs will be identified.

☺ Small-class size was beneficial in serving mainstream educationally challenged students. I was able to allow myself one-on-one instruction time as well as whole-group assessment. There was more time in the day to do hands-on lessons, projects and crafts that align with the curriculum. (Teacher)

☺ The small class size was very helpful to me this year because I had educationally challenged students who needed a little more time and attention. The class size enabled me to do group work with those students while the others worked. Also, I could identify the needs of each student and assessment was made quickly. In a full-sized class of 25 students I could not identify student learning problems as quickly. (Teacher)

Table 6.10 shows that 30% of all STAR K students were in S, 35% were in R, and 35% were in RA. The percentages of males and of females in S, R, and RA classes are essentially the same as the percentages of total students in each class type, confirming STAR's random-assignment process. This similarity is also true for the percentage of non-special-education students in the classes (30%, 35%, and 35%). However, of students identified as needing special education help, 36% were in S, 33% were in R, and 31% were in RA. Of these conditions, the RA result is most troublesome. Apparently, in RA classes teachers send inattentive or bothersome students to be with the teacher aide, who is less likely to identify a student's special needs than is the teacher. In S, the teacher must deal with all students without an aide, and thus is likely to identify a student's special needs. Procedures for identifying and teaching special-needs students may be an important area for staff development.

☺ An elementary school psychologist in southern California expected class-size reduction to result in far fewer referrals for special education. Instead, the number of referrals actually went up in his large, urban school. Teachers found that they had more time to fill out the lengthy forms. They could find more time to attend school study team meetings, and they reported feeling that they had time to learn more about their students with special needs. Teachers also felt that they had a better opportunity to implement the individualized strategies that were suggested, typically, by colleagues on the study team.

TABLE 6.10 Differential Identification of Special Needs Students by Class Type

	Percentages of STAR Kindergarten Population In Categories						
	(S)		(R)		(RA)		
	(%)	Dif.[a]	(%)	Dif.	(%)	Dif.	Total
Total (N)	30	—	35	—	35	—	100
Male	30	—	34	−1	36	+1	100
Female	29	−1	35	—	36	+1	100
Total (N)	30	—	35	—	35	—	100
Identified							
Sp. Ed.	36	+6	33	−2	31	−4	100
Not identified							
Sp. Ed.	30	—	35	—	35	—	100

[a] Dif = difference. This is the percentage difference between observed and what might be expected, considering the distribution of all students (N) into the three class types. Proportionately more students get identified as needing special education help in S than in R and especially in RA.

Student Gains in Success Starts Small (SSS)

Although SSS was primarily to observe the differences in teacher and pupil behaviors in classes of 15:1 and 24:1 in two matched schools, the students were tested twice (December 10 and March 29) so there would be assessment information for Title I requirements. Results of the testings were reported in normal curve equivalents, or NCEs. Both schools had a "schoolwide" Title I program, but School A had small classes and School B followed a pull-out design. The focus of SSS was Grade 1. School A had four Grade-1 classes averaging 15:1; School B had two classes averaging 24:1 and one split-grade class (K–1) with 10 Grade-1 students. To be included in the SSS analysis, a student needed both a pre- and a posttest on the California Achievement Test (CAT) total reading subtest. School A had 56 of 61 students (92%) with both scores and School B had 47 of 57 (82%) students with both scores. School A had an average pre–posttest NCE *gain* of 14.3 for students in 15:1; School B had an average 8.7 NCE gain for students in 24:1 (Achilles, Nye, Zaharias, & Fulton, 1995; Table 6.8, p. 39).

Although comparative data between Schools A and B were not kept on student discipline problems defined as student referral to the office, descriptive data for three years at School A for Grade 1 show a decrease in referrals (38, 28, 14) even though at Grade 1 enrollment was relatively constant (63–60 students). In the first year of the comparison, students had regular-sized classes. In year two, they had small classes in Grade 1 only. By the third year, students had experienced small classes in K and in Grade 1, and total referrals were at 14, down from 38 two years prior. The behaviors showing decreases were disrespectfulness (6 to 2), refusal to do work (9 to 1), disruptiveness (8 to 1), hitting/fighting (12 to 7), and stealing (3 to 0). (There was an increase (0 to 2) in weapons, but in 1993–1994 a teacher had to report any student with any weapon, including very small pocketknives that had previously been allowed.) The changes in behaviors suggest that students were doing their work, getting along better in class, and learning what is expected for school success. Increased test scores supported the behavior changes in the 15:1 classes.

☺ Small class size has leveled the playing field for all children. *All* children have the opportunity to be honored every day. Each child's academic and social growth has increased due to the prescriptive teaching that meets individual needs. The "small-class-size" experience has decreased student misbehavior and enhanced the achievement of limited English proficient (LEP) students and exceptional learners. (Educator)

Student On-Task Behavior and Discipline

Student benefits identified by Evertson and Folger (1989, pp. 8 and 10) included that "small classes had more students on-task and, conversely, ... fewer students off-task than the regular class. Also, students spent less time waiting for the next assignment" and "waiting for teacher's help" in the small classes. Evertson and Folger (1989, p. 10) also noted that "regular classes were rated higher in inappropriate behavior."

On-task and engaged behavior should result in improved student outcomes and, one hopes, in development of positive school behaviors that will last into later grades both to improve learning and to reduce indiscipline. After viewing videotapes of teachers teaching in small classes, Robert Egelson developed the following observations. Here is the summary in Egelson's own words.

I was trained as a school psychologist. I have a Master of Arts degree and am licensed to practice psychology in the state of North Carolina. I have worked for the past 18 years as a staff psychologist, and have worked for the past 5 years as a child psychologist for a local mental health center. I have consulted on hundreds of cases of children with various diagnoses including Learning Disability, Attention Deficit/Hyperactive Disorder (ADHD), Autism, Developmental Disability, Traumatic Brain Injury, Attachment Disorder, Anxiety Disorder, Behaviorally/Emotionally Handicapped, and Conduct Disorder, etc. Many of these consultations have occurred in the classroom. I have observed children in dozens of classrooms, in all grades and settings. I also am the father of two children (ages 13 and 11), and have volunteered weekly in their school since they were in kindergarten.

Recently, I had the opportunity to view a videotape of children receiving instruction from their teacher. The videotape had been taken in a school from an economically deprived neighborhood, in a small town in Western North Carolina.

A majority of the students are reported to be from lower-income homes. The children are in four classrooms described as "Reduced Class Size" classrooms. The tape specifically showed children in 1st, 2nd, and 3rd grade classrooms. In each classroom, the children are receiving instruction from a teacher, and the primary form of instruction is oral, requiring the students to concentrate using their auditory abilities, but especially to pay attention. Each classroom is shown on the tape for approximately 30 minutes of instruction, and in each classroom the children are seated at their desks or on the floor.

What is significant about these classrooms is that the children are rarely distracted. They concentrate on the teacher's presentation in a way I have never observed before. What stands out dramatically is that none of the four teachers had to prompt a single child to pay attention, or to stop bothering another student or stop engaging in off-task behaviors, for the entire instructional session (approximately 30 minutes). In one classroom, I did not see any of the approximately 15 children look away from the teacher. They didn't even look out the window for a moment for the entire session. In fact, it struck me that if I were to videotape children in classrooms that I have been in, they would have paid attention; but after 10–15 minutes, they would exhibit some off-task behaviors. This caught my attention. In most classrooms that I have visited and observed (1st through 3rd grades), the teachers must prompt some of the children to pay attention at least every 5–10 minutes.

I began to ask questions. How many children in the school with the "reduced class size" were diagnosed with ADHD? How many children are referred to a psychologist due to behavior problems? How well do the children do on academics? While it has not been possible to answer definitively the first two questions, the answer to the third question was that children had gained as much as a full year's added academic achievement over the 3–4 years that the reduced-class-size project had been in place. In other words, children who might be expected to be working at the 2nd grade level were working at the 3rd grade level based on end-of-year testing.

It also became obvious that two other things are happening in this school. First, when children first begin to attend this school in kindergarten, like most children, they will look at the older children's behaviors and will imitate them. In this school, they will imitate paying attention, focusing carefully on the teacher's instruction. They will not imitate off-task behaviors or behaviors that result in conduct problems. Second, the teacher is free to spend much more time focusing on academics rather than on disruptive behaviors. Over the course of an aca-

demic year, this must surely help explain the gains in academic achievement. It appears from this observation that
the "reduced class size" concept is the cause for the dramatic changes. I hope that this will be carefully studied
both in terms of causation and outcome in other settings
(possibly in other pilot projects in other school districts),
and in terms of academic vs. behavioral improvements.
(6/28/98)

The on-task behavior in small classes described here by Egelson
helps validate the time-on-task results reported in SSS (Achilles et
al., 1994; Kiser-Kling, 1995) as well as the improved behavior and
achievement outcomes explained in other studies. Finn (1998) explained that inattentive and withdrawn behavior in classrooms is
more often displayed by difficult-to-teach students who may seem
distracted, preoccupied, or to be daydreaming, and who may give
responses not related to questions asked. These inattentive students
do not participate in even basic schooling efforts (responding, doing
assignments, turning in homework) and "are even less likely than
disruptive students to be directed to constructive learning activities"
(Finn, 1998, p. 21).

The time-on-task differences favoring small over larger classes
obtained in SSS (Achilles et al., 1994) and the observations expressed
by Egelson show that in small classes there is considerable student
engagement and participation. Small classes may keep a student engaged in class activities and "make it difficult for a teacher to over-
look the needs of a particular student" (Finn, 1998, p. 20).

☺ I had 12 kindergarten children with no assistant this
year. Last year I had 15 first graders and that was a won-
derful experience. This year did not go as well, perhaps
because of the particular children: one EMH child with
a 53 IQ, two children who missed being placed EMH by
2 and 3 points, one child with severe behavior problems
(violent), and two children who were *very* immature and
not yet ready for kindergarten. Kids like this need more
adult supervision than available even in a 15:1 class.

Yet, are these findings new or surprising? Hardly. Cooper (1989) summarized outcomes of prior class-size studies, including those findings of Glass and Smith, Cahen et al., Education Research Service, and others, and found essentially what has been reported here. Some of Cooper's findings summarized on Table 6.11 show positive nonacademic gains that in the long run may be more important than test-score gains.

Smith and Glass (1979, p. 46) explained what nonacademic changes occurred for students as follows.

Class size affects pupil's attitudes, either as a function of better performance or contributing to it. In smaller classes, pupils have more interest in learning. Perhaps there is less distraction. There seems to be less apathy, friction, frustration.

Studies, such as SSS and STAR, and anecdotal reports point out that student behavior, as assessed by discipline referrals, greatly improves in small classes. Student participation in and identification with schools increase in small classes.

The Class-Size and School-Size Nexus

Research has consistently demonstrated a generally deleterious effect on student achievement and behavior of larger schools (Cotton, 1996; Fowler & Walberg, 1991; NASSP, 1995). Seldom do researchers have the opportunity to explore this issue *within* a carefully controlled experiment. Using STAR data, Nye (1995) undertook a school-size and class-size study. In STAR, researchers established class sizes randomly within certain parameters. Some classes grew out of these class-size ranges slightly as the study progressed, but the numbers of children in classes were known. The students and teachers were assigned at random. Each school contained all three class-size conditions: S, R, and RA. The schools in STAR ranged from 329 to 1,070 students (Nye, 1995, p. 160).

Using student achievement on standardized tests as the criterion variable, Nye analyzed the STAR R class results in the schools of varying sizes using correlation techniques. In the STAR control group or the R classes averaging 25 students, Nye determined a decreasing student test-score performance as school size increased.

In R classes, 12 of 14 correlations were negative, a significant finding ($p \leq .05$). The negative correlations ranged from $-.03$ to

TABLE 6.11 Summary and Paraphrase of Student Benefits (from Cooper, 1989a, pp. 85–87)[a]

A. Small Classes Improve Student Academic Achievement

- Small classes improve pupil achievement (math and reading) in early primary grades
- Lower academic ability pupils benefit more from small classes than do average pupils
- Positive benefits accrue more to economically or socially disadvantaged pupils

B. Students in Small Classes Get Positive Nonacademic Gains

- Attitudes toward teacher and school
- Self-concept   • Mental health
- Motivation   • Participation
- Discipline and behavior

---

[a] Cooper cited meta-analyses and other studies in deriving the conclusions (e.g., Glass & Smith, 1978; Educational Research Service, 1978, 1980). The findings reported by Cooper were later obtained in STAR and STAR-related studies (e.g., SSS study in NC).

−.30; and 9 of the 12 negative correlations (75%) were −.12 or higher. Nye found 10 of 14 correlations negative in S classes (not significant), and those negative correlations ranged from −.01 to −.19, with only 3 of 10 (30%) above −.11. Even in S classes, the negative relationship between school size and class size remains. The relationship, however, is far less pronounced than in the larger schools, and it is not statistically significant.

Although we probably won't demolish all of the too-large schools and replace them with smaller ones, we can grant a double benefit to the many students in large schools by providing small classes for them. These youngsters will reap all the benefits of the small-class effects plus the added benefit that their small classes will overcome the generally negative effects of the larger school on their school performance.

Just as cluster and pod plans, looping and school-within-a-school processes can make a big school seem small for middle and high school students and give them a safer environment with greater participation and increased achievement (e.g., McPartland, Jordon, Legters, & Balfanz, 1997), so can small classes provide similar benefits for elementary students.

Size matters in education, and small size matters big time for small students.

Summary

As material in this chapter clearly shows, small classes offer students many benefits, especially disadvantaged and minority students in early grades. The advantages are far more than just increased test scores. Better identification of students who may need special help, increased student participation and engagement, decreased behavior problems, and reduced retention in grade are all part of benefits to students. These same outcomes may also provide social and economic benefits that will help repay the initial investments in small classes for the benefit of young children. Table 6.12 summarizes student benefits from some class–size studies used as a base for this text. The many benefits are easily noted. What other single treatment provides these many positive outcomes for young students? Class size is administratively possible. Let's put kids first, finally, by getting class size correct.

TABLE 6.12 Summary of Small-Class Benefits: Source Study (x = yes, as included in the source named)

Observed In-Class Changes	Lind-bloom	Olson	Glass & Smith	Smith & Glass	Burke Co.	SAGE	SSS	FCPS	Cooper	STAR	Project Success	Teacher "Stories"
A. Increases												All
• Time-on-task		x	x	x	x	x	x	x	x	x	x	
• Hands-on	x	x	x	x	x	x	x	x	x	x	x	
• Indiv. attn.	x	x	x	x	x	x	x	x	x	x	x	
• Diagnosis	x			x	x	x	x	x	x	x	x	
• Social climate	x	x		x	x	x	x		x	x	x	
• Management	x	x	x	x	x		x	x	x	x	x	
• Participation	x	x	x	x	x	x	x	x		x	x	
• Academics	x	x	x		x		x	x	x	x	x	
• Parent involv.					x					x	x	
• Early ID of spec. ed.										x	x	
• Morale	x	x		x	x		x		x	x	x	
• Space					x		x			x	x	
• Enrichment	x	x			x		x	x	x	x	x	
• Text/methods	x	x			x		x	x	x	x	x	
• Group work	x			x	x		x	x		x	x	
B. Decreases												All
• Indiscipline	x	x		x	x		x		x	x	x	
• Retention										x		
• Spec. ed.										x	x	
• Stress	x	x		x	x		x			x	x	

a SSS, Success Starts Small, Achilles et al. (1994); Kiser-Kling (1995); SAGE, Student Achievement Guarantee in Education, Molnar (1998); Project Success, Achilles et al. (1994); FCPS, Fairfax County (1997).

7

Teaching in Small Classes: Incentive and Reform

Whether classes are large or small, teachers must make them work as well as they can. What do we know about what teachers do in small classes, or do differently in smaller and in larger classes? Do teachers view small classes as a valuable means to the end of student achievement? Are small classes an incentive for better teaching? Answers to questions like the following will help sort out some facts and myths about small classes.

1. What is the *incentive value* of small classes? Do professionals get their primary incentives from tangible things, such as salary, or from other things?

2. Do teachers need extensive professional development before students benefit from small classes?

3. Did successful teachers of small classes get the small-class skills, attitudes, and knowledge that they demonstrate in their small classes from their regular preparation programs, in staff development, or both?

Teacher Benefits: Small Classes as Incentive

In the continuing tension between an education process and the "business model," there is discussion of incentives to improve education. Some advocate bonuses for high-performing schools or merit pay for teachers. As an alternative to the business model of incentives, especially cash and bonuses, consider an education-as-profession proposition for small classes as an incentive:

- Small classes are an incentive for teachers AND an immediate bonus for students; they serve the teacher and offer direct benefit to the client.

As described in more detail elsewhere in this text, at the end of each year, the Project STAR research team conducted almost 1,100 interviews with teachers and teacher aides over STAR's four-year duration. Two interview questions for over 230 teachers during the last year of STAR (1988–1989) were the following:

- If you had your choice, which teaching situation would you choose:
  __ A small class with 15 children OR __ A regular class with 25 children and a full-time aide?
- If you had your choice, which teaching situation would you choose:
  __ A small class with 15 children OR __ A $2,500 salary increase? (Word et al., 1990, pp. 193–194)

Compared to a $2,500 salary increase or a regular-sized class with a full-time aide (RA), teachers understood the incentive value of small classes (S). For responses to both questions, teachers overwhelmingly selected S, although there was some variation associated with the class size that the teacher had the prior year. For example, 81% of respondents who had S chose to have S rather than a regular class with a teacher aide (RA), and 71% who had R chose S over RA classes. The *second* question about a $2,500 raise could clearly be considered a question of choice between two *incentives*. This survey was in 1988–1989 when teacher salaries were lower than in today's marketplace. Of respondents who had the S condition, 70% chose S rather than RA; 63% of RA teachers would elect S rather than the $2,500. Detailed results appear in Zaharias and Bain (1998, p. 17).

Do results from 1989 on teacher perceptions of class size as an incentive still hold true? Ten years later, Jean Krieger, Assistant Principal of the National Blue Ribbon Award-winning Woodlake Elementary School in Mandeville, Louisiana, decided to test out the idea. She became encouraged to do that during a discussion with a state representative. The extra cash incentive was less than STAR's $2,500, but nevertheless, enough to be a potential "incentive." Here's Jean's story.

Interview Story

When visiting the state capital recently, I had an opportunity to talk with a state legislative representative. We had a pleasant conversation beginning with my question of "What do you think is the most important issue in primary education?" The representative was a bit surprised at my question, but she answered that the issue of pupil/teacher ratio was of concern. I asked then if she knew the difference between pupil/teacher ratio and class size. She said that she was a bit unsure and asked that I explain it to her. I told her that the pupil/teacher ratio was sometimes a figure contrived using the total number of certified personnel working within a school facility to aid in the instruction of children and that class size was the total number of students found in a classroom with one teacher throughout the day. I said, "When I enter a classroom and count how many children are with one teacher and are on her roll as students she teaches daily, that is the class size." I explained the disparity between those terms and how people misunderstand them. The representative then questioned me about teacher preferences. She told me that she is often petitioned by union representatives and school board personnel to vote for a pay raise for teachers. She said that when questioned, this group always considers a teacher pay raise to be the best use of funds. She expressed that she would love to question teachers and hear their opinions. I told her that I believed that all of the primary teachers (grades kindergarten, one, two and three) whom I knew would eagerly prefer a guaranteed lower class size of no more than 18 children (under most any conditions) instead of having a $1,000 pay raise. (The state legislature was proposing a budget which included such a raise for teachers.) I invited her to visit our school where she would be able to interview teachers privately to question them.

Later I asked the faculty about their choice of having the promised $1,000 a year pay raise or a guaranteed lower class size. All of these teachers said that they wanted the lower class size. I went to a public primary school in our district where the class size had been lowered to 14–20 in each kindergarten and first-grade class through the use of Title I funds. As I privately questioned the teachers, I found that they were unanimous in their desire to have the lower class size instead of a raise even if their counterparts in high school chose to keep the larger class sizes and opt for the raise. These teachers were most anxious to tell me their thoughts about class size.

Play STAR's $2,500 incentive out at the secondary level with one hypothetical situation that could easily be factual. Suppose an English teacher meets 120 students per day in either five or six classes. Is it unreasonable to expect this teacher to average at least 10 minutes per week per student correcting student essays, papers, quizzes, and tests? The math is uncomplicated: 10 minutes per week times 120 students is 1200 minutes or 20 hours per week, or half of the work week of many nonprofessionals who make higher salaries. This 10 minutes per student, which most likely is a low estimate of the time required for a teacher to provide student feedback, does not include planning time, professional meetings, staff development, or school-related activities such as attending sports or social events. If there are 40 weeks of school and 20 hours (minimum) of extra time are spent on student papers and tests, that is 800 hours per year for $2,500. The math isn't difficult. The $3.13 per hour is far below minimum wage. A teacher would prefer fewer students.

This crass calculation presumes, however, that primary motivators for teachers are extrinsic. Weld (1998) put this into perspective. He connected his incentive idea to the motivation theory of Herzberg (1966), who would call teacher pay a "satisfier," but not a "motivator." The important distinction is that "low salary can lead to dissatisfaction among teachers, but merit-based pay and bonuses are not a source of greater motivation for good educators" (Weld, 1998, p. 33). This is Weld's story, and he should tell part of it in his own words. Weld (1998, p. 33) clearly is describing class size, even though he does use student–teacher ratio and class size as synonyms at one place.

The research evidence suggests that funds intended for recognizing outstanding teachers (and for inspiring others to strive for excellence) would be better spent by helping dedicated teachers dismantle the barriers to achieving intrinsic rewards.... Rather, job motivation among teachers is related directly to intrinsic matters: recognition, responsibility, and achievement of goals linked to the work itself. A 1994 study by the National Center for Education Statistics identified a number of impediments to teachers' goal attainment. Chief among them was the *issue of large class size*. The single most important action schools can take, therefore, on behalf of a cash-based public mandate to improve schooling, would be to reduce the student-teacher ratio (sic) in classrooms. *Not only would this improve teacher motivation by increasing the likelihood of intrinsic rewards, but the benefits for children in smaller classes would be dramatic as well* (emphasis added).

Educators deserve realistic extrinsic rewards, but once reasonable extrinsic-reward conditions are met, intrinsic rewards become motivators for teacher improvement: student success, work conditions that allow the teacher and student to succeed, the job itself. Having time to teach, to know the students, and to watch them achieve education outcomes are the incentives that small classes provide, and incentives that most teachers prefer.

☺ A first-grade teacher in Southern California was delighted to discover that making out report cards was much less cumbersome with the advent of CSR. Not only were there fewer grades to decide, but she realized that she really knew her children much better. The smaller number of children had allowed her to complete a variety of assessments over time. She could get around to several students each day to take running records of their oral reading. Instead of working on report cards for two days of the weekend, she was finished in one day. Her report-card comments were more thoughtful.

☺ A second-grade teacher reported that standardized testing was a different experience this year. The past practice of testing a half class at a time was abandoned with the smaller class size. This year, the atmosphere was relaxed and the entire class was tested at one time.

A pay-driven incentive may work at the low end of the motivation-for-improvement scale for educators, but even if it did, it could hinder student success even while serving as a source of teacher satisfaction. Applying the business-world idea of cash incentives for performance in education could produce the following situation. Successful schools get extra funds as a reward for success. They can use the funds for faculty bonuses or for school support to become even more successful. Schools judged not successful get no bonuses or extra help, the notion being that to provide extra help only rewards mediocrity. As Cooley (1993) and others have demonstrated, the schools judged not successful on traditional measures of test-score outcomes tend to serve high-poverty children who stand to benefit most from extra resources and the small classes that are incentives for teachers.

Extra-resources-and-pay incentives may work in some businesses, but what about in other conditions? Consider a military confrontation. If a fighting force under an Army commander is losing its engagement, would the commander assign extra amounts of limited resources to another unit that is winning and deny these resources to the hard-pressed unit that is losing its battle? Is education more like a war on ignorance or like building widgets on an assembly line?

> ☺ A first-grade teacher is pleased to see how much farther various supplies have stretched with the advent of smaller class sizes. She will never escape having to purchase materials with her own money, especially for science and art. She sees that her dollar has gone farther this year.

Although all teachers and students deserve the quality that small classes bring, at a minimum, small classes should be targeted to help teachers and students in high-poverty and low-success schools. After a nationwide study of small classes, Wenglinsky (1997, pp. 24 and 25) concluded that "fourth graders in smaller-than-average classes are about a half a year ahead of fourth graders in larger-than-average classes ... the largest effects seem to be *for poor students in high-cost areas*" (emphasis added). Teachers who work in small classes often explain that they are "working harder but enjoying it more." This is a common way to explain an intrinsic incentive.

Professional Development and Teaching Performance

Training is one way that professional people remain on the cutting edge of their fields and share their successes and problems with others in the field. Few would doubt that good staff development helps both successful and less successful teachers improve. Continuing personal and performance development is one characteristic of professionals, and may be a type of incentive for some teachers.

Few would argue that staff development is an attribute of a professional and a path to improvement in one's chosen field. On the other hand, there is debate about whether teachers must have staff development before they can teach in small classes and get a small-class effect. The distinction between teachers doing things *differently* or doing *more of the same* touches on this topic. Is more different? Do teachers need lots of new professional development in order for small classes to benefit their students? Some class-size critics contend that class size matters little or not at all without staff development. What does the research to date say?

Without widespread experience with small classes, it is not clear what staff developers would teach the new small-class teachers. With so few small classes to study, how have staff developers determined what the teachers need? In the many class-size studies that have already demonstrated measurable student benefits, did teachers have small-class specific professional development? The answer to this question is a definite "No." Yet, some things were different in small classes as determined from interviews, questionnaires, vignettes, observation, and student outcomes. Teachers did more of the same successful strategies that they had been using all along and students in smaller classes demonstrated improved outcomes. However, as in larger classes, some teachers in small classes were "better" than others if student test scores were the primary criterion of goodness. In STAR, all teachers were certified for the grade level they were teaching. This condition may *not* be true in all small-class situations, and especially where there were teacher shortages before class sizes were reduced. Surely by studying successful teachers of small classes, staff developers can learn what can speed up other teachers to become better teachers in small classes. Absent evidence to the contrary, and based upon the evidence compiled for this book, consider the following propositions:

> Teachers in small classes did not have specific staff development . . . yet students achieved more, and behaved better.

1. Most teachers don't need staff development to teach successfully in small classes.
2. Sound teacher preparation programs provide teachers with what they need to know to be good teachers, but large classes stifle or negate the effective use of good teaching methods. Small classes let teachers use effectively what they already know. Said another way, good teacher preparation produces

teachers who can drive 60 mph, but society provides roads that only let them go 40 mph.

3. Small classes for a teacher's first few years of teaching would provide new-teacher induction, and small classes may be an incentive to retain good teachers in teaching.

4. Research points clearly to one area of staff development needs for teachers: identification of and working with special-needs students.

Nothing in these propositions suggests that professional development doesn't help teachers teach better. If done correctly, staff development keeps the teachers alive and vibrant. The electrifying nature of knowledge growth requires that teachers stay current, but just learning new knowledge and skills is not enough. Teachers also have to be able to use the new information.

> Large classes prevent teachers from doing what they know how to do.

Education's Triage Method

When overwhelmed and rushed, especially in crucial situations on a battlefield or in horrific disasters when they receive many casualties in a very short time, medical professionals can't effectively use best medical practice on all clients. They employ triage as best practice under the worst conditions. In medical triage, the professional makes an immediate decision about the potential for a seriously injured or ailing patient to survive. This decision helps the professional stretch scarce resources of time and materials so that those who may benefit from professional treatment or from scarce medicine will get the resources. Victims least likely to survive are given the available resources and are made as comfortable as possible, but they are provided few services until those most likely to survive are cared for first.

The triage metaphor may be repulsive in education, but is it farfetched in many of today's schools? Consider one teacher with 30 or more very young learners whom the teacher cannot serve well or equally. Best education practice requires that teachers work individually with each child, start where the child is, diagnose and remediate problems, and help the child improve. Yet, there is nearly relentless social and political demand and hype to have all students be above average, *and to do it now, if not sooner*. If the teacher cannot get all students to the goal, does the teacher use the scarce resources on those most likely to reach the goal to get the average score higher? The triage decision may be based upon the "injuries" students have received on the battlefield of life: poverty, fetal-alcohol syndrome, abuse, and past performance (Cooley, 1993; Snyder & Achilles, 1996–1997). The small-class context gives the teachers more time, space, and resources per child to help all children succeed. Small-class success stories overwhelmingly describe the opportunity and ability to work with all students.

Teachers' sense of "burn out" driven by trying to serve too many children in too little time, or from the rushed "finger in the dike" approach to teaching everything to all, is not uncommon—and it is emotionally devastating to some sincere educators. Small classes offer teachers relief from to this emotional dilemma, too. The list of incentives for improved professional performance of good teachers is served well by small classes.

The Conditions of Teaching:
Small Classes Yield Big Results

According to Darling-Hammond (1998, p. 6), part of the three-pronged central message of the National Commission on Teaching and America's Future included these two elements:

- "What teachers *know* and *can do* is one of the most important influences on what students learn. . . .
- School reform cannot succeed unless it focuses on creating the conditions in which *teachers can teach and teach well*."

Darling-Hammond (1998) listed conditions that influence teacher success. Of those listed, at least 13 elements reported in the late 1990s are similar to important ones that had been isolated in the 1960s and reported in Lindbloom's (1970) analysis of small-class activities.

Lindbloom found that in smaller rather than in larger classes the following 10 things took place more often (paraphrased):

1. Frequent individualized instruction was geared to the needs and interests of students.
2. In addition to the textbooks, teachers used a wider variety of educational materials to enrich teaching.
3. Increased interaction occurred among pupils and between teachers and pupils.
4. Teachers made greater use of innovative or new materials and methods.
5. There was more student self-control and discipline with less teacher domination.
6. There was more small-group work than in larger classes.
7. Improved human relations occurred among students and with the teacher.
8. A greater number of instructional activities were used frequently.
9. Fewer discipline problems were observed.
10. There was improved morale among teachers.

Teachers in smaller rather than larger classes personalize their instruction more, use a wider variety of methods and materials, have more student participation, and experience fewer discipline problems.

More than 25 years later, Darling-Hammond (1996, pp. 6–11) reported the following elements that contribute to teacher success:

- Work in environments that allow them to know students well
- Induction of beginning teachers (mentoring)
- Communities in which students are well known
- Structures that allow teachers to know students and their families
- Teachers have enough sustained time with their students each day and over the years

- Personalized teacher–student relationships
- Greater knowledge of students' learning styles
- Performance-based assessments
- Accelerated and in-depth learning approaches
- Stronger connections between the classroom and students' homes
- Opportunity to adapt their instruction to the needs of their students
- Positive changes in students' educational performance as well as their own working conditions

---

> Conditions that foster good teaching also foster learning. Small classes are the foundation for these conditions.

This commentary emphasizes the need for more and better prepared teachers and upon restructuring schools so that teachers can teach. According to substantial experimental evidence, many benefits that the National Commission seeks in schools flow directly from small classes.

Political Correctness and Child Advocacy?

Teachers and parents know that the items on both lists describing the conditions and elements of good teaching are important for student learning. The lists were compiled nearly 30 years apart. They represent what most would simply call "good teaching" and what teachers learn in their teacher-preparation programs before they enter teaching. They hardly represent skills usually learned only in staff development. The parallels between the two sets—one set developed from class-size studies long ago and the other identified by a recent National Commission—raise questions that deserve attention in a serious research agenda.

How much of the operational agenda of the National Commission on Teaching and America's Future could be achieved primarily by reducing class size? If many conditions of good teaching can be achieved solely by small classes, leaders could redeploy funds normally used for staff development to hiring qualified teachers. Benefits would go directly to the student and avoid the vendor. Some staff developers might become classroom teachers, thus reducing class size and meeting a National Commission concern of "reducing the numbers of nonteaching staff and increasing the numbers of classroom teachers" (p. 11). Allocation of teaching roles gets at the distinctions, described earlier, between class size and PTR.

> Classroom teachers comprise 60% to 80% of education employees in European and Asian countries studied by the Organization for Economic Cooperation and Development, but only 43% in the United States, where the number of administrative and nonteaching staff has more than doubled over the last 30 years. (Darling-Hammond, 1998, p. 10)

The issue of deployment of educators raised in this quotation and also by the class-size and PTR distinctions addressed by Miles and Darling-Hammond (1998), by Achilles, Finn and Bain (1997–98) and Achilles, Sharp, and Nye (1998), and in other places shows how clarity about PTR and class size is important in education discussions. Small classes for young students aren't immediately "politically correct," but they are great for kids. (Sigh.)

Small classes for young students aren't immediately "politically correct," but they are great for kids.

Projects Versus Learning Communities

The project-driven nature of American education helps explains the PTR and class-size conundrum, too. Our prototype pupil, Pat, may leave the regular classroom for special help in the basics of education, such as reading. Who now is responsible and accountable for Pat's reading progress? A "special" teacher and the regular teacher both teach Pat reading; the PTR changes, but not the class size in Pat's regular classroom. How do the regular disruptions in Pat's day disturb Pat, the teacher, and other students, *and* deprive Pat of time-on-task?

> Discussions of "class size" have been confounded by lack of class-size data and by use of PTR data to try to negate class-size effects.

Teachers in small classes are *responsible and accountable* for the learning outcomes of the students in their classes. In a small class, the classroom teacher can address many of a student's learning needs. When students in small classes are not pulled out of class for remediation or special projects, the teacher and students form a learning environment where the teacher can employ professional knowledge of teaching. The teaching day is not shattered frequently by students coming and going and adding commotion to the normal business of 15–18 people learning together.

Direct Benefits to Clients; Indirect Benefit to Adults

In many respects, students, who are the primary clients for public school education services, are very low on the education food chain; children are the plankton deep in the education sea. The feeding frenzy for benefits from limited education dollars occurs toward the top of the food chain where the adults reside.

> **Children . . . are very low on the education food chain.**

Whenever a new fad offers its silver-bullet remedy to the arsenal of projects claiming to solve education problems, money flows to adults, but not usually even to the classroom teachers who, themselves, are only part way up education's food chain. Experts, developers, consultants, peddlers, project pushers, publishers, staff developers, evaluators, and others are first in line with their hands out for education-improvement funds. Class-size change presents an entirely different matter. Small classes are a sure-fire shot for education improvement, and the class-size benefits go *directly* to the pupil. Might this help explain why class-size change gets lukewarm support from some educators who are not full-time classroom teachers?

Pockets of resistance to class-size change remain among teachers themselves. Because the research shows that students should do better in smaller classes, teachers will now be more accountable and visible if there are few gains after class sizes become smaller. Some teachers argue that they can do well in a large class with a full-time aide, regardless of the research evidence on student-benefit outcomes with the use of instructional aides. Inclusion and English as a Second Language needs, however, may make this claim more legitimate than when STAR was conducted.

Teachers who want to know what to do in smaller classes can get plenty of help, if this knowledge will make them more comfortable in accepting their small-class roles. The knowledge is wrapped into studies of teachers in small classes where students have done well. Lindbloom's (1970) listing of good teaching and learning practices that occur more frequently in smaller than in larger classes is one of many summaries of research-based successful practices in smaller rather than larger classes.

The teachers in the Filby et al. (1980) study did not have specific staff development to prepare them for their new small-class role. The change to small classes just happened: *"General patterns of change occurred when class size was reduced ... classroom management* seemed easier and more effective ... *classes functioned more smoothly, student attention rates* were generally higher, and there were *fewer absences"* (emphasis added).

Class-size changes in South Carolina required some shift in personnel. Not only did a teacher have a smaller class, but the teacher might teach at a new grade level, and this could require adjustments. Sheldon Etheridge, a Title I director in Berkeley County, South Carolina, shared the following story about a new small-class teacher at a new grade level.

To enhance learning opportunities for 5-year-old kindergarten (K) children, federal funds were used to reduce class size from a state-funded half-day K program staffed at 30:1 to a full-day K with a class size of 20 students. Nearly 100 students who enrolled at a rural Title I school site were tested with a nationally recognized and developmentally appropriate test prior to school. The teacher selected for this class had never taught K. A long-time first-grade teacher, she stated that she "decided to teach the kindergarten children what they had to be prepared for to be successful in the first grade." The absence of staff development to obtain the stated outcomes is note-worthy. Here is the story.

> ☺ A district-level early childhood coordinator employed the same year as the K program was piloted was able to visit and participate with the class several times during the first half of the school year. Assisting with class lessons, observing displays of student work, and noting the parental support for classroom activities made it evident to the coordinator that the K teacher held high expectations for her selected group of students.
>
> Not being involved in the student selection process, the coordinator knew only that the students in this class had been specially selected. Student performances, class responses, and the classroom activity level led the coordinator to assume that high-performing students had been selected for supplemental services. It was after midyear before she realized that the lowest-performing students had been selected.
>
> Scores had been prioritized from low to high with parents of the lowest-performing students being contacted first. They had been asked to agree to their child receiving extended services in a small class. All students in this class were tested at the beginning of the 1st grade using a cognitive skills assessment test, and all (100%) performed "ready" for 1st grade. The school percentage of all 1st-grade students obtaining this measurement level was 62.4%.

The material presented here strongly suggests that with small classes teachers can do more and better those teaching practices that they already know how to do. Analyses of what successful teachers do in small classes may help provide staff-development ideas and materials to assist other teachers in getting up to speed in small classes more quickly. As more teachers have experiences in small classes, their stories of success and failure will begin to develop a knowledge base of the practice of teaching in small classes. What teachers actually do in small classes has been the subject of several chapters in this text. The question of small classes as an incentive for teachers is more than hypothetical. Evidence presented in this chapter supports that class size, not minor cash bonuses, is a powerful motivator for good teachers. That is the professional way.

When a vaccination to deter polio was perfected, professional practice and public perception required that the vaccination be made available to all young children. Similarly, a long stream of research shows benefits of small classes for students. The use of small classes should be as much part of a professional educator's preventive practice as vaccination is a part of a doctor's professional preventive practice for polio or other childhood maladies.

Whether or not educators can use small classes as part of professional practice depends much upon public policy and public perception.

8

Public Perception and Professional Practice

Is class size important when adults are choosing a college for their children? Why do adults go to small seminars rather than mass meetings for important things? Why do committees divide into subcommittees for crucial tasks? Do most adults use data and re-search results when making personal decisions? Understanding of the class-size effect is part of an educator's knowledge. Use of the data on class size is part of a teacher's professional practice, but how—or even if—a teacher uses that knowledge is partly a function of public perception and policy. Public perception and professional practice are two key variables in establishing policy, creating change, and improving education for children.

The 1998 recommendation by the President of the United States to provide funding for more teachers and to get class sizes to a manageable and workable size met not only with political differences and priorities, but also with considerable media interest, and not all of it was positive. Notably, many print and electronic me-dia stories featured negative responses about using small classes for small children. Criticism and doubt came both from people out-side of education and also from some educators, strange as that may seem.

Some headlines grabbed America's attention as President Clinton attempted to focus part of his education platform to help children. On the one hand, the lack of positive education headlines and media fixation upon crime, violence, politics, and economics tell much about America's interest in children. On the other hand, the lack of educator enthusiasm for improving education by using research results tells much about an interest in doing business as usual, with little thought about how to use data and knowledge to improve education. Without studying possible options for implementing small classes, some administrators could only see increased costs; some teachers could only see that one teacher might have fewer students than another. In the American spirit of exploration and entrepreneurship, where were stories of successes, possibilities, promise—even the correct representations of years of research? Here are some headlines:

"Educators Wary of Clinton's Plan to Trim Class Size" (*Toledo Blade*, 2/8/98)

"Small Classes: Popular but Still Unproven" (*Education Week*, 2/18/98)

"Old Education Reform Idea Recycled" (*Greenville News*, 2/25/98)

"Education Falsehoods" (*Savannah Morning News*, 3/6/98)

"The Education Wars" (*The National Journal*, 3/7/98)

"Does Class Size Matter?" (*US News and World Report*, 10/13/97)

"Smaller Class Sizes Fail to Help Most Students" (*Detroit News*, 11/2/98)

"Do Smaller Classes Mean Better Schools? Economists Aren't So Sure" (*The Chronicle of Higher Education*, 4/3/98, pp. 17–18)

Maybe some economists were not so sure about education processes and outcomes. Did many economists foresee the fall of the Berlin Wall or the decline of socialism, predict the Dow Jones Average reaching 8000, or diagnose the "Asian Flu"? Maybe a second opinion is reasonable here! Generally, parents, some educators, and even some politicians are more convinced about the positive value and effects of smaller classes than were some economists. Many stories under these negative headlines contained outright inaccuracies, such as the statement about STAR that appeared in the *Detroit News* item: "The results were insignificant except for kindergartners."

Public Media and Professional Constraints

The media express public perception and people may use media to try to sway public perceptions. In trying to influence public perception, advocates may use facts and data, half-truths, or even inaccurate information. Sorting fact from opinion challenges a well-educated citizenry. Inaccuracies can occur when media report old information that has been superseded by new studies or more powerful research methods, or when writers use secondary sources without checking them for accuracy.

Media can handle news in positive, negative, or neutral ways. For example, the *USA Today* reported 50-year results of the Framingham Heart Study positively, expressing its benefits and featuring comments by the present study director (Haney, 1998). Contrast that with a 9/30/98 unsigned editorial in the *Wall Street Journal* that included half-truths ("The STAR study found that class size indeed might matter—in kindergarten") and inappropriate comparisons of class size and PTR. An article in the *Weekly Standard*, (3/9/98) featured questionable and unsupported opinion: "No reform is more expensive than smaller classes," and "there's a simple reason why small classes rarely learn more than bigger ones: Their teachers don't do anything differently".

Half-truths and errors might be good for discussion, except they may get picked up as "true" and repeated in other media outlets as authoritative. Apparently, once something gets reported, the item must be "correct." Media releases even carry questionable comments such as "first, the conventional wisdom that students do better in small classes is flat wrong" (Finn & Petrilli, 1998). This unsupported comment tries to blow away actual research findings from over 20 years and the knowledge of parents and teachers in exchange for uninformed opinion.

Contrast the license of mass media with the process to get research into publication. Before major studies are released into scholarly journals, they are carefully reviewed by recognized scholars. This time-consuming process of peer reviewing is called *refereeing*. Large-scale studies such as STAR may be reanalyzed before widespread release. STAR data have been analyzed by researchers both in America and abroad. These researchers and analysts have confirmed STAR's results in scholarly reanalyses and review.

In addition, using what they learned from the STAR Project, researchers have replicated STAR on a smaller scale and each of the replicated studies provided results similar to those obtained in STAR. One frustrating part of the scholarly and conservative approach to getting accurate data and results into the public domain is that the "nattering nabobs" who noisily proclaim that class-size research is wrong are not required to provide any evidence. When that ill-informed opinion gets spread in the media, as if true, who suffers? Young children suffer. Ouch.

Except for the political spin on tobacco, what research is as poorly presented in the public media as the research on class size? People disregard research on ways to help children with about the same disdain as dismissing research on the detrimental effects of tobacco by saying, "My grandmother smoked three packs a day and lived to be 100!"

Professional Evidence and Anecdote

When she was president of the National Association of Elementary School Principals (NAESP), Yvonne Allen, Principal of the Whiteville Elementary School in Whiteville, Tennessee, told of her school's success achieved through the use of small classes. Although Whiteville Elementary was not in Project STAR, the faculty reduced classes in K–3 to about 15:1, and reduced class sizes in Grades 4–8 some with the help of Title I funds. Whiteville was a rural school whose students were 79% minority, 85% on free or reduced-price lunch, and 45% from single-parent homes. Here's a synopsis of the results, as told by Allen (1998, p. 2) in her column.

☺ Instead of purchasing material and equipment, we employed additional teachers to reduce class size, and the benefits were outstanding. With smaller classes, our school achieved the following:

- Higher test scores
- Increased mastery of basic skills
- More materials covered in class
- Increased parental involvement
- More parental contact and home visits
- Fewer discipline problems
- Improved self-esteem
- Increased school attendance

In 1993, Whiteville Elementary School (once known as the "graveyard") was recognized as a Blue Ribbon School of Excellence. Without the Title I program and reduction in class size, I do not think we would have received this recognition. Years later, when Title I funds were reduced, teachers were cut, and once again class size in Grades K–8 increased. All the accomplishments mentioned above were diminished.

When added to STAR and other large-scale class-size efforts, anecdotal evidence like the Whiteville story adds credibility to the research evidence of the value of small classes (15:1) for small children. The heartbreak in Principal Allen's story is what happened when funds were reduced so that larger classes became the norm again. While sitting in their offices far away from "the maddening crowd" of the work world of schools, education's critics may claim that "money doesn't matter," but maybe they should spend some extended time in elementary schools with student populations like Whiteville's—there are plenty around!

Rather than starting a discussion of improving education and helping children by denigrating years of research, where was the media balance and inquiry that might seek answers to such questions as the following?

- What research is the basis of the class sizes we now use?
- What research shows that small classes harm students?
- Where small classes are presently in use: (a) How were they implemented? (b) How were they funded? (c) How much more do they cost? (d) What are the positive and negative issues surrounding use of small classes?

What institutes or "think" tanks invited class-size researchers and teachers to discuss the issues? What class-size researchers and practitioners testified in formal hearings to present the recent class-size research and practice in education? Why did the media rely upon old studies and polarize the issues rather than embark upon intellectual and balanced discussions? Consider two comments heard in class-size disputes that are appealing and seemingly logical on the surface.

- Would you rather have your child in a big class with a good teacher or in a small class with a poor teacher?
- Class size won't make a difference unless teachers do things differently; if you do what you've always done, you'll get what you've always gotten.

In relation to the first "logical" position, whatever happened to the other options? What about preferring to have your child in a small class with a good teacher, or in a large class with a poor teacher, or any of the gradations between? The polarized positions of good/poor teacher and large/small class are useful to guide a discussion only if people realize that teachers are not just "good" or "poor," but that there are many levels of variables such as knowledge, aptitude, skills, etc. between "good" and "poor" as absolutes. Figure 8.1 shows the outline of the discussion.

In Figure 8.1, quadrant I (small class, high-quality teacher) is clearly preferred to quadrant IV (large class, low-quality teacher). What about quadrants II and III? Which is to be preferred? On what variables or to what degree? Under what condition? How do we know? What research needs to be done here?

The second "logical" positions may be true if group size by itself has no impact or effect on student outcomes, but an impact has already been shown in numerous studies.

TEACHER (Ability, Training, Quality (etc.)

		Good or High	Poor or Low
CLASS SIZE	Small	I Best Condition	II ?
	Large	III ?	IV Worst Condition

Figure 8.1. Polarization of Class Size and Teacher Quality

Recall that Cahen and Filby (1979, p. 494) reported that even then, people were commenting that "reducing class size will have no effect if teachers do exactly the same things in a small class as in a large one." Change of public perception and acceptance of new data are difficult and take time.

Small Class Size: Common Sense and Good Research

If you were a parent of a kindergarten (K) child, would you ask the principal to put your child in a larger class? Why might you choose to home-school your child or to send your child to a private school at considerable personal expense? If you were a teacher, would you request more children in your class? As an adult, you know that for very young children and *especially* for your child, at least, smaller class size is better for the early school years.

Public perception of "small is better" among people who study education is strengthened by at least three reassuring phenomena that support the idea: (a) research and evaluation results of small-class education activities; (b) common sense; and (c) practice not only in education but in other areas (such as business with its concept of span of control). Table 8.1 shows some parallel reasons for expecting a small-class effect. For example, few people question the use of tutoring or one-on-one intensive education work to help a youngster. One-on-one is the ultimate small class. Some occupations employ apprenticeships during which new entrants learn the field's

TABLE 8.1 "Common Sense" Examples From Practice, and Research and Evaluation Results Favoring "Small is Better" in Schooling

---

A. "Common Sense" Support for Small Classes

> Parent comments: Do parents ask for *larger classes* for their kids?
>
> Home schooling, private schools, tutors, mentors
>
> Annual poll results (e.g., Phi Delta Kappa)
>
> Teacher comments: Do teachers request *more* students in their classes?

B. Practices in Education and Other Fields: Prior Research Reviews

Reviews	*Research and Projects Supporting "Small Is Better"*
Lindbloom (1970)	STAR, LBS, Challenge
Olson (1971)	Success Starts Small (SSS)
Glass & Smith (1978)	Indiana's Project Prime Time
Education Research Service (1978, 1980)	Burke Co., NC; Downtown School
Cooper (1989)	SAGE; Fairfax County
Robinson (1990)	Cooperative Learning, Peer Tutors, etc.
ERIC-CEM (1994)	
	Business/Industry/Government
	Span of control client focus
	Decentralization apprenticeships

C. Samples of Research and Evaluation Results Supporting Small Classes

Remedies Using Small Classes	*Projects Using Small Classes*
Special education	Reading Recovery (RR)
Vocational courses	Success for All (SFA)
Gifted and talented	Privatization, charter schools
Advanced placement	
Remedial projects	
Pre-school (Head Start)	

knowledge and skill base. Many businesses, government agencies, and military units employ hierarchical organization models and spans of control where one adult supervises the work of 6–10 other people who, presumably, can read, write, feed themselves, and use toilet facilities with no help. (Consider the kindergarten teacher!)

For many reasons, people use small groups for important tasks, including communication patterns in the small groups, and to benefit from group dynamics of small groups. In education, small groups allow teachers to diagnose problems and take corrective actions, provide individual attention, monitor output, and correct homework and tests to help with student cognitive and skill performance in schools. But all crucial early education outcomes are not cognitive. Children need to get along with others and to become socialized. Children need to like school, become engaged in school, and begin to identify with school and learning as fun and useful. Children in small classes develop a positive affect toward education during the early grades (Finn, 1993; Finn & Cox, 1992; Smith & Glass, 1979; Voelkl, 1995). Why should schooling at any level, but particularly early school experiences, be conducted in large classes? Examples in Table 8.1 show that many adults and young students with special needs thrive in small groups. Public perception and practice for adult tasks and learning are far ahead of public perception, policy, and practice for early public-school education.

A Solid but Flexible Foundation

Effective class sizes offer nothing short of a potential revolution in improving America's education system. When education critics speak of rebuilding or reinventing education, it's clear that this rebuilding must start in the very early grades, as any major construction effort must rest upon a solid foundation. The class-size change in working conditions in schools adds not only incentive for teachers, opportunities for children to learn, renewed interest on the part of parents in the education process, but also the chance for educators to develop a solid and unified education process leading to lifelong learning. To begin this journey, education leaders and policymakers must seriously consider *how* the education system must be redesigned. There is no single and simple way to educate people for the future, but there surely can be better ways.

Research on class size has provided useful, replicated, anecdotal, and experimental evidence that smaller classes assist teachers in teaching and students in learning. Applying what is known about small classes offers promise for the redesign of an education system that has rapidly come to resemble a tired and worn-out inner tube with hundreds of splotchy patches. Given the dynamic nature of education's contexts and challenges, education as an inner tube always being patched in different places whenever some problem bursts out, is dysfunctional. Our young people can't go places fast in a vehicle with flat tires, tires that are ready to blow out, or tires designed to support a lighter, slower conveyance from times past.

There is solid, replicated, experimental evidence that smaller classes assist teachers in teaching and students in learning, especially in early grades.

Equally important to public perception of the education process, however, educators must be professional scholar–practitioners in the eyes of the public. Rather than debate the tired question, "Is education a profession?," educators can operationalize professionalism by employing substantial research-based knowledge of education in their regular practice. What demands on education does the requirement for professional practice make?

Education as Professional Practice

Educators have claimed that education is a profession. How does knowledge of the class-size effect fit into professional practice? There are differing determinations of what constitutes "professional" and professional practice. Here's one idea, using class-size knowledge and its application as part of the example.

Basically, persons in a profession work on "people problems." They have clients. At a minimum, a profession has a research-driven and consensually validated knowledge base that professionals apply in their work with clients. The knowledge base that constitutes the field's basic skills and information is not necessarily predictable, and most assuredly it is not immutable. The education knowledge base is in a state of flux because of changing contexts, demands, and advances in practice. The efficacy of a field's method of inquiry provides a way to access, advance, and assess the knowledge base and its applications. Unfortunately, unlike medicine, education has few true experiments to contribute to its knowledge base.

A profession has standards of conduct and application, including a code of ethics that establishes requirements that the profession holds for its members. A profession has generally accepted entrance criteria that may be formally established by licensure and certification. As persons practice in the profession, they become more adept at intellectual decision making to solve problems brought before the profession. That is, they gain an understanding of informed professional judgment (IPJ) that comes from advanced study and from reflective thinking about practice. Other elements that help define a profession include a common language, steps toward self-regulation, the notion of guided entrance into the field such as an internship or working with a mentor, and personal and public attributes such as the public's perception of the work and the workers. Table 8.2 contains one set of criteria that help explain the concept of a profession as the term is used here.

A professional is not limited to working in the private sector. For example, a lawyer can be in private practice or might work in the government. The idea of a "bound" profession means that the professional works under public regulation and receives basic compensation from public sources, such as taxes. Simply put, where the person practices the profession does not determine whether or not the person is a professional. Location of practice does influence, however, some control over the individual's ability to carry out informed professional judgments. A "bound" professional may not be free to use all aspects of a knowledge base because a public governing board sets policies about what a person whom the board employs can or cannot use freely.

Nevertheless, the professional must make choices about applying one element or another of the knowledge base to serve clients. Thus, if the school board sets class size in K–3 at 28:1 and provides funds for that level, the educator in that district is formally bound by that class size. The educator is professionally responsible, however, to work toward obtaining class sizes that the research has established as good for the students. This is also part of IPJ.

TABLE 8.2 Characteristics That Define "Profession" and Serve as a Base for Decisions About Competence in the Practice of the Profession

A. At a Minimum a Profession Has Certain Required Elements:

- A body of knowledge (knowledge base or KB) that the professional uses to address client (people) problems. This KB constitutes a field's *basic skills* and information.
- A method of inquiry or way to advance, assess, and access the KB and its applications. (Use of the KB is not predictable or immutable.)
- Standards of conduct and application (code of ethics), e.g., Oath of Hippocrites. "Primum Non Nocere" (at least, do no harm).
- Entry requirements (licensure, certification) and internship or some guided practice before full licensure.
- Intellectual decision making based on "informed professional judgment" (IPJ factor).
- Self-regulation
- Common language
- Others (?)

B. Desired Elements of a Profession or a Professional

- Continuing education to maintain and advance the field
- Introspective/reflective practitioners
- Public perception of quality and value of the field's KB
- Personal perception (attitude) of professional and evident self-respect
- Effective communication
- Pay for service
- Flexibility

Elementary-grade class size fits into the model of decisions made by a professional who works in the public sector and is bound by public policy. Although the research supports that young children, especially in early primary schooling, profit more from being in classes of 15–18 youngsters with one teacher rather than in classes of 25 or 30, a public-policy decision may not support the small class sizes because of conflicting ideologies, costs, policy priorities. **The core issues of the concern for class-size decisions are the following questions.**

  (a) What is the knowledge base?
  (b) How strong are the data upon which the knowledge base rests?
  (c) How will the knowledge base get applied?
  (d) What will be the benefits for clients (students, society)?

Nevertheless, what educators do can be analyzed to ascertain how well the profession accepts the knowledge base or information its members use. For example, a well-established tenet in education is that people learn in different ways. This idea incorporates research results from many disciplines, and from the works of such people as Gardner, Sternberg, Feuerstein, Vygotsky, and others. Educators would agree that this knowledge is well established. On a scale of 1 to 5, where 1 is a high degree of certainty and 5 is a low degree of certainty or a low amount of evidence to support the assertion, educators would probably say that the concept "people learn in different ways" would deserve a rating of 1. In practice, this knowledge may be translated into teaching styles, arranging classrooms to accommodate learning centers and student learning styles, individualizing instruction, etc. The knowledge that "people learn in different ways" leads the educator to use teaching strategies that address differences in ways that students learn.

In the case of class size or of a "class-size effect," a test of professional knowledge and use similar to the fact that people learn in different ways is appropriate. The assertion is that, in general, smaller classes provide better learning opportunities than do larger classes, especially for children in their early years of formal schooling. The class-size statement may not be quite so accepted as the idea that people learn in different ways, but it can still be supported.

As shown in Table 8.3, education's knowledge base can be analyzed in varying degrees by specifying the research upon which a knowledge-base element is built and then by assessing the degree of certainty about (in this case) the class-size effect. Four examples of education's knowledge base, including class size, are analyzed in Table 8.3. Consider how this analysis can be applied to education practice such as retention in grade, use of homework, early intervention,

TABLE 8.3 Assume That Education Is a Profession. What Is Its Knowledge Base (KB)?

1 *What Is the KB?*	2 *Built or Based on?*	3 *How Sure?*[a]
A. People learn in different ways.	Gardner, Sternberg, Vygotsky, Feuerstein, Thorndike, etc.	1
B. Retention in grade seldom helps the client.	Years of study; meta-analyses (e.g., Holmes & Matthews, 1984)	1
C. Early intervention helps students later in schools. K is valuable.	Head Start, Perry pre-school, many other studies	1
D. Class size (e.g., 18:1 in early grades) influences student outcomes.	STAR and related work; current class-size studies; some early studies and meta-analyses	1
⋮		

[a] 1 = very positive; 5 = almost no empirical evidence.

and value of kindergarten. That the idea of professional practice has been neglected in education is, unfortunately, found in articles such as Glickman's (1991) "Pretending Not to Know What We Know," or even more disturbingly, in everyday observations of the contexts, policies, and practices in many American schools.

> **The research supports that young children ... in early primary schooling ... profit more from being in classes of 15–18 youngsters with one teacher.**

Why Haven't Educators Used Research-Based Ideas Freely?

One explanation for why some educators do not use what the research shows is that public education is a bound profession. Not employing some of the knowledge base may also be attributed to low certainty or consensus about a knowledge-base statement; that is, the idea gets a low rating such as 4 or 5. This situation is common with new knowledge that is still being evaluated. Perhaps the educator does not understand or know this knowledge, or know how to use it. If the person does not know and therefore does not use education's established knowledge base, professional development is one alternative.

In a less positive scenario, the person may know but not use some of education's knowledge base. In an established profession such as medicine, this could be called malpractice. The analogy is not as far-fetched as it might first seem. When a professional (in this case, an educator) makes a decision for a client (in this case, a student), the choice that the educator makes should rest on the profession's knowledge base and standards of conduct. At a minimum, a practice must not harm the client (i.e., the student).

Concepts of Profession Applied to Class Size in Schools: A Comparison to Health

When an adult makes a personal choice, a different situation is at play. For example, results of the Framingham Heart Study that began about 1948 helped people understand influences of food and lifestyles on health, and particularly upon coronary heart disease (CHD) and cardiovascular health. Today, food packages contain labels with nutritional data. Adults may read those food labels carefully, control the intake of fats, and heed the warnings on tobacco products. Personal decisions and public policy on health issues evolved as the adults considered and applied the knowledge gained from the Framingham Heart Study and from other studies of human health.

> **Extensive study of class size has provided evidence of a positive link between class size and student outcomes ... with approximately twice as many participants as were in the Framingham Heart Study.**

The long-term and extensive study of class size has provided evidence of a positive causal link between class size and student outcomes. The most comprehensive class-size study is a longitudinal experiment with approximately twice as many participants as were in the Framingham Heart Study that led to observable changes in Americans' health behaviors and habits. STAR and STAR-related studies have provided evidence on class size that is similar in importance for educators to the evidence provided for health professionals on CHD and cardiovascular health by the Framingham Heart Study. The Framingham Heart Study resonated with adults, and adults made choices to help adults. In the case of applying STAR information, educators and other adults must make choices for young people who do not vote. Very young children in their first years of schooling also do not have the freedom of choice about schooling that adults have about their lifestyles. In this respect, educators have a special relationship with their clients, the young students in their care.

STAR ... studies have provided evidence on class size that is similar in importance for educators to the evidence provided for health professional on ... cardiovascular health by the Framingham Heart Study.

Let's Start With Professional Practice

This discussion emphasizes two main phenomena: public perception and professional practice. Educators have little direct and immediate influence on public perception, so they are advised to work on professional practice as a way to improve education, influence public confidence in education, and begin to influence the public perception of education. A bold first step is to use a professional knowledge base that derives from research and that supports the concept of profession as shown in Tables 8.2 and 8.3. Improved professional practice can lead to improved public perception of education, and to increased confidence in education.

The use of small classes in Burke County, North Carolina, is an example of improved professional practice leading to altered public perception of education. Educators and school board members cautiously introduced small classes in a pilot-test mode using local funds and including provisions for stringent evaluation. As positive

results were accruing and parents and teachers were providing anecdotal evidence of successes, evaluators provided "hard data" such as
test-score gains. Public discussion and debate aired various positions
on the issues. Continuing positive evidence of the efficacy of small
classes as sound professional practice eventually prevailed to influence public perception. Voters supported the small-class effort with
increased local fiscal support and school leaders accepted the challenges. Student achievement increased in comparison both to prior
years and to the rest of the state.

Although the county is not wealthy, support for small classes is
strong. Class sizes in Grades 1–3 average 17:1, and the community is
now considering how to support small kindergarten classes. Results
of professional practice have strongly influenced public perception
leading to public support for the demonstrated results of practice.

Improved professional practice should provide observable evidence of what is required to obtain the benefits of professional practice. This evidence can be described. In the case of small classes in
education, one area for observing and describing the benefits of practice is to consider what teachers do in small classes. Other chapters
have described how teachers apply professional knowledge in small
classes that themselves are good professional practice.

9

Needed:
World-Class Ingenuity

No matter what instruments he uses, at some point he reaches the edge of certainty beyond which conscious knowledge cannot pass.

(Jung, 1964, p. 21)

Are the calls to restructure, reform, redirect, and reinvent education simply rhetoric? The concepts "small is better" and "less is more" that are the heart of small classes for students offer educators great opportunities to initiate the "systemic change" so often expected or demanded by education's critics. When presented with the opportunity to implement small classes, leaders' responses have frequently been more of the same, rather than using the class-size mandate as a lever to creativity. Anguished cries abound: "We need to hire more teachers; we need more school rooms; it won't work without massive staff development; we've always done it this way before; it's too expensive." Sure, it will take work, but.... To paraphrase a favorite criticism about teaching in small classes, "If we do what we've always done, we'll get what we've always gotten." It's the leaders' turn to make class size right.

Small-class research and small-class mandates could be the pistol shots at the starting line in the race for divergent thinking about ways to sprint education out of its Rip Van Winkle lethargy. Mostly, though, the excitement and enthusiasm about small classes may die in a flurry of business-as-usual retreats or be bushwhacked by opportunistic claims that "something must be better, so let's wait awhile. After all, we have not yet tried all possible options." Complacency detests challenges.

Granted, potential innovations and opportunity for systemic change surrounding class size would require diligence, energy, vision, industry, and leadership. Perhaps doing class size in new ways would require creativity, changing some rules, regulations, and laws, but any *potential* risks to clients—students—would be offset by the immediate benefits of smaller classes. Because no research has shown any negative effects of small classes for students, teachers, or parents, leaders who choose to use the positive results of small-class research will not put any of education's clients or personnel at risk. Their risk taking should be limited to criticisms they may receive for selecting class size over other options, to political and ideological disagreements, and to the ways that they may select to implement the small classes. Several questions point to the generally threat-free environment for electing education improvement through use of small classes.

1. What research or theory supports the presently used class sizes?
2. What popular education idea or project either does *not* depend on small classes for its effect, or would not be improved in a small-class setting?
3. What substantial rebuilding does not require a firm foundation upon which to build? Primary grades are education's foundation.

Frequently heard reasons why *not* to consider smaller classes for America's youngest students include the following:

1. There is no research evidence that small classes are better than what we have, and what research there is provides mixed results. (Wrong)

2. We need more classrooms and they are not available. (Maybe) The ones we have need repair before we add new ones. (Possibly true)

3. We need many more teachers. They are not available, and even if they were, we can't afford them. (It depends. Consider PTR vs. class size.)

4. It is just too expensive. (Wrong)

5. We can't expect improvement by class size alone; we need staff development, technology, etc. Fill in the blanks depending on the current fad. (Wrong)

Below are point-by-point summary responses to some wailings about why small classes can't be done. The details and research base for the summaries are discussed throughout this text.

1. No Research Evidence, or Inconclusive Research Results

The hard-line advocates for research who offer this line of argument might also ask, "Where is the research evidence for the class sizes we use now and have been using?" Early class-size research results were inconclusive for many reasons described earlier. The single biggest problem with inconclusive "class-size" research is that it is not class-size research, but research on pupil-teacher ratio (PTR). The work of Glass and Smith (1978) helped sort out some reasons for the early confusion. Project STAR provided experimental evidence of the small-class effect that Glass and Smith identified.

Beginning with Indiana's Prime Time statewide project, carefully implemented large-scale class-size projects and studies have provided consistent positive results as in, for example, the DuPont study (Bain et al., 1988a, 1988b); SAGE (Molnar, 1998); Burke County Studies (Achilles, Harman, & Egelson, 1995); Success Starts Small (Achilles et al., 1994); "Life in First-Grade Classrooms of 1:14 and 1:23 Class Size" (Kiser-Kling, 1995); the STAR/LBS/Challenge studies; *STAR Follow-up Studies* (Bain et al., 1997); The Fairfax County Evaluations (Fairfax County Schools, 1997); and *When Money Matters* (Wenglinsky, 1997). See Table 1.1, p. 18 for a listing of STAR and some related class-size studies, 1985–1999, that provide consistent class-size results. Anecdotes and observations provide examples of small-class successes. The Downtown School in Winston-Salem, North Carolina, offers class sizes of 14:1 at the same per-pupil expenditure as in other buildings in the system. Narratives from California's Class-Size Reduction or CSR, and summaries such as Finn (1998), McRobbie, Finn, and Harman (1998), and Pritchard (1998) add to the growing crescendo of support for small classes in early primary grades.

Now that research approaches and methods are improving, the class-size effect is found consistently in research and evaluations, especially in well-designed studies conducted at sites with careful class-size implementations. Class-size critics concede a class-size effect even as they argue that "something" must be better, or speculate that use of small classes "will dilute the quality of the teaching force" or that "suburban districts will recruit the best teachers away from the inner cities" as reported in Hoff (1998, p. 5). Well, this dog doesn't hunt either, for two reasons. Inner cities usually don't get the best teachers, but small classes in both inner cities and suburbs will help level the field and be an incentive for teachers to stay in, or even go to, the inner cities. Have people forgotten Bloom's (1984a, 1984b) early and substantial research on mastery learning and tutoring, the ultimate class size of 1:1?

2. Classroom Shortages

Reducing class sizes will require more space, but the key concept here is space, not classrooms. Is it written in stone that all early primary classes must be in schoolrooms and school buildings as currently defined? Unquestionably, huge numbers of education facilities are in horrendous condition. These shoddy buildings need repair or replacement, but eroding facilities—like the "off budget" federal debt—is an adult-perpetuated unfunded liability sloughed off on children who don't vote. Fix the facilities. Secure the needed spaces. Create small-class sites. This task won't be easy or without critics. If anyone thinks that one district has it bad, consider the statewide problem in California with its headlong rush to reduce classes in Grades 1–3, rather than phasing in one grade per year.

☺ The upper-grade teachers are mad, as a second-grade teacher reports. They are not happy with the inequity of

> having anywhere from 32 to 36 kids and a longer school day. The additional classrooms needed for class-size reduction have made their conditions worse, taking up precious playground space and using up the multipurpose room and its stage. The quality of their school has diminished, in many of their views. At one nearby school, the school library was even lost to a "CSR" (class-size reduction) classroom.

Classrooms in traditional schools are expensive when they are accompanied by other special-purpose spaces: cafeterias, auditoriums, laboratories, media centers, gymnasiums and locker rooms, teacher lounges, etc. But, if primary outcomes of early elementary schooling in Grades K or pre-K, 1, and perhaps Grade 2 are such things as learning to read and literacy, learning numbers and numeracy, learning to get along with others, and learning the required routines of schooling, must spaces in which students achieve these basic competencies be in traditional school buildings? Can suitable spaces for early primary education be found in other sites that can be connected to a "home-base" school via technology? If the spaces can be located near the clients or in the students' neighborhoods, parents and volunteers can get to the sites easily, thus increasing parent involvement and, perhaps, decreasing transportation costs. Consider spaces in down-sizing businesses, libraries, public buildings, YMCA/YWCA, churches, club houses in subdivisions, store fronts and malls, and in overbuilt office complexes. Prerequisites are safety, sanitation, security, small classes, and a successful teacher. Satellite classrooms provide flexibility and reduce crowding elsewhere.

A school building is an immobile investment. "Found" space is flexible. When population shifts, new spaces or satellites can be sought. By moving K–1 or K–2 *out*, those schools will have more spaces and rooms for programs and students in the upper grades.

If portable or "relocatable" classrooms truly are portable, why are they always found on school grounds? Consider innovative approaches to locating K–1 sites in neighborhoods. Place the portable on church or other grounds. Let the new "partner" use the space on weekends in exchange for utilities, or ground-lease costs.

☺ A space story or, more exactly, 11 stories.

I was presenting class-size ideas to educators in a roomy, comfortable space that adjoined a kitchen and dining area. This setting had space for 3–4 classes of 15–18 primary youngsters. The space was used later in the day for meetings, recreation, etc., but early in the day it was idle—except for meetings like the one I was conducting.

The space was on the ground floor of a high-rise. The upper 11 floors housed retired educators! Consider the potential of *this* setting for small community-based K–1 classes: volunteers to tutor children with problems, adults to join children at lunch, or to read stories to children—11 stories of volunteers *on site*.

3. We Need More Teachers

Smaller classes and growing enrollments do require teachers. Futurists explain that America has exited the Industrial Age and is entering the Information and Knowledge Ages. If true, this paradigm shift will thrive on new investments in education. Besides the new investment ideas, however, the concept of redeploying education personnel based upon the demonstrated benefits of small classes offers one way to address the "problem" of too few classroom teachers.

American education is presently a project-driven hodgepodge of pull-outs, special programs, and state or federal initiatives conducted by specialists and support personnel. Darling-Hammond (1998, pp. 10–11) pointed out that in the United States about 43% of education personnel are classroom teachers, 23% are institutional staff such as supervisors and principals, and 34% are other administrative and support personnel. Research also shows a large difference between PTR and class size (e.g., Achilles et al., 1998; Darling-Hammond, 1998; Lewit & Baker, 1997; Miles, 1995). This difference between PTR and class size offers one arena for negotiating small classes.

Small classes by themselves provide many benefits that "special" projects are designed to provide. Judicious redeployment of project teachers and use of Title I funding for schoolwide small classes could reduce the need for new teachers and alleviate the problem of temporary-certificate teachers that followed California's crash implementation of small classes. New teachers will be needed, but surely not the huge numbers that some people have predicted. Consider these new teachers a social investment in the Information Age and a pledge to help young children become lifelong learners.

Using site-based-decision-making educators might determine the redeployment of personnel through professional discussion and study. The "worksheet" provided as Table 9.1 can be modified to help a faculty at a specific site explore how redeployment of existing personnel and the benefits of small classes may intersect. If small-class benefits would replace much of the Title I need, or eliminate retention in grade (etc.), how many current "special" teachers could become directly responsible for students as "regular" classroom teachers?

Small classes attract parents. Parents as volunteers can replace paid teacher aides. Small classes let teachers work closely with the volunteers so teachers and volunteers are successful. Small classes pose a problem here, too: smaller classes equal fewer parents.

☺ Parents still can't help at school very often, according to a first-grade teacher. With a class of 30 students, there were usually one or two parents who could become the "room parent" and others who could help out on occasion. With class size reduction, the population to draw from narrowed. It was hard to get one consistent parent to participate and help out.

The example in Table 9.1 shows 19 regular teachers and 12 "special" positions, counting all other persons (except the secretary) and counting the 4 teacher aides as 2 possible teachers. There are approximately 19 + 12 "positions" to serve the 511 students. If all positions were converted to "regular" teachers—not a real scenario, of course—there could be a class size of 511 divided by 31 positions or 16.5. However, the target class size of 20:1 would require 26 "regular" teachers, and that would leave 5 "special" positions, such as administrator, media/library, etc. (Numbers in parentheses in

TABLE 9.1 Worksheet: Conversion of Current Staffing Into Options for Class-Size[a] (Examples are in Parentheses)

	Positions (n)	
Current Staff Allocations	Actual	Desired
I. Regular classroom teachers	(19)	
II. Teacher aides (est. 2 per teacher for conversion)	4 = (2)	
III. Specialty persons		
A. Media/library	(1)	
B. Guidance	(1)	
C. Administration	(1)	
D. Specialists		
1. Language(s)		
2. Phys. ed.	(.5)	
3. Music/art	(.5)	
4. Technology	(1)	
E. Title I, etc.	(2)	
F. Exceptional children		
1. Gifted	(.5)	
2. LD	(.5)	
G. Other (nurse, coordinator)	(2)	
H. Total specialty personnel	(12)	
Total positions available for consideration (19 + 12)	(31)	
IV. Total enrollment for consideration	(511)	
V. Lowest class size for consideration (511 ÷ 31)	(16.5)	
VI. Negotiated target to achieve	(20:1)	

[a] Adapted from Hansel (1997), Principal, Draper Elementary School, Rockingham County, NC.

Table 9.1 are the examples.) In a careful analysis of needs vs. benefits of small classes, the total faculty in a school could offer alternative staffing combinations to meet the needs of students that the school serves.

4. It's Just Too Expensive

A couple of common expressions seen in advertisements or on bumper stickers sum up the cost issue: "If you think that education is expensive, try ignorance" or "Pay now or pay much more later." As long as education is seen solely as an expenditure, its cost is reported in present-time outlays. But education is properly considered an investment and seed money for the growth of human capital. The actual return on education makes education a productive investment, and the potential social-benefit returns like less vandalism or violence, reduced teen pregnancy and unemployment, and fewer dropouts are education's equivalent of the miracle of compound interest.

Creative approaches to implementing small classes have promise of cost containment. Table 9.2 shows some areas of potential cost savings that follow the careful implementation and evaluation of small classes. The long-term benefits of small classes such as reduced retention in grade, improved choices of advanced courses in high school as preparation for higher education, school behavior, reduced violence and vandalism, higher academic grades, and school participation are future benefits and not immediately recognized. Early identification and remediation of learning problems may save long-run special education costs. The costs of small classes depend on implementation, trade-offs, and creativity.

5. We Can't Expect Improvement by Class Size Alone

Actually, improvement by small classes alone is exactly what the research says: class size is a key variable in student outcomes. "Do small classes in and of themselves affect student learning? Yes is the answer that emerged from Project STAR" (McRobbie, Finn, & Harman, 1998, p. 1). Staff development did not improve STAR outcomes (Word et al., 1990). The positive class-size outcomes in the studies reported here have been obtained without special staff-development work.

Small classes facilitate teachers doing what they learned to do in their teacher preparation but were hindered from doing effectively because of the sheer numbers of students in classrooms. Inability to use freely good education processes has become a serious problem

TABLE 9.2 Checkpoints for True Costs of Reasonable-Sized (e.g., 18:1 or so) Classes in Primary Grades[a]

Item	Potential for Cost Saving
A. Grade retention	• Number of students held back decreases • Later drop-out rate decreases
B. Improved student behavior in school	• Vandalism costs decrease • Required corrective actions, such as Saturday school or detention, decrease • Classroom disruptions decrease
C. Remediation and special projects	• Fewer expensive special projects required • Concentrate on fewer students intensely for shorter duration
D. Early ID of learning problems	• Special education programs reduced in later years • Programs accurately "targeted" to most needy students • Note possibility of increased costs in K and 1
E. Teacher morale	• Increased attendance • Reduced substitute costs • Reduced "burnout"
F. Creative space use	• Transportation-related costs • Flexibility and "found" space • Partnerships with business
G. Community, parent involvement, volunteers	• Small classes attract parents and volunteers • Field trips (etc.) are less congested

[a] Reproduced, with permission, from Achilles and Price (1999), "Can Your District Afford Smaller Classes." Reprinted with permission from ASBO International, Reston, Virginia.

because of changing demographics that other research has shown to make educator's tasks more difficult (e.g., Cooley, 1993; Hodgkinson, 1985, 1992). If technology should finally show positive results in improving student outcomes, will hordes of kids be using one computer, or will one or two students be working at each station? Small classes make other education processes and treatments work better. What special project in education relies on large classes for its effects?

Small classes in K–3 are one answer to pervasive problems that seem to keep American education from receiving acclaim and world-class status. Education's tires are spinning on glare ice trying to get education out of a snowbank. Rather than adding snow tires or giving education a push, education's critics are trying to shovel the glacier with charters, vouchers, home schooling, privatization, or untested projects.

A rising tide of expectations for education is both true and healthy. Education can have many benefits. Small classes should be the nonnegotiable foundation. Choices can come *after* education's basic foundation and structure are strengthened. This is a value choice. Depending upon *how* smaller classes are implemented, they may cost very little more than present expenditures. If so, that will leave considerable education funding to be used for other things that the clients request. One thing seems clear. Whatever the "other things" are, they should be received better by a better rather than a less well-educated citizenry.

Education's successes compound educators' problems. Through education, more and more people can read and communicate. The numbers of people attending some form of formal education are increasing. With their acquired thinking and communication skills, successful people request educators to provide more and better education services for their children than they received. This keeps education moving ahead. Thinking people pose problems for tradition and complacency. The next demands for education improvement will be far more educated than the last. This includes parents' requests for smaller classes for their children.

Implementation Tasks and Choices

The first decision about class-size research is whether to believe and use it. Given the consistent and positive results of class-size studies, this should be a *pro forma* choice. Most districts are already using some form of class-size presence, if only in special classes for specific purposes. A choice to *expand* using class-size effects has logical antecedents, based on present levels of small-class effects for special purposes.

As decisions to implement small classes in early primary grades are debated, *major* concerns will be costs, personnel, and space. Key questions will center around "how to" and policy issues: how to accomplish small classes, what to evaluate and how, potential "trade-offs," how to use the small-class base to leverage systemwide improvements, and other policy questions. In keeping with the "individualized" nature of education, implementation of small classes is likely to be different in different places. In the absence of any single, simple master plan, the answer is "it depends." Implementation steps will depend upon many context factors in each state, district, and site.

Research, theory, and examples—case studies, really—of exemplary practice all provide ideas and guidelines. Some decisions will depend upon philosophy and values—value-driven leadership. Based upon research, theory, and practice, implementation might approximate the following model.

I. The student should *start* schooling in 15:1 in a full-day kindergarten, or in Grade 1 in 15:1 if there is no kindergarten. Research (e.g., STAR) supports 15:1 in K–3.

   A. First year of small classes → K and/or Grade 1.
   B. Add Grade 2 the second year.
   C. Add Grade 3 the third year.
   D. Project Challenge showed very few benefits at the end of third grade from one year of small classes starting at Grade 3. Small classes are more preventive than remedial in K–3. Start in K and move up one grade per year.

II. Study and evaluate the year-to-year results of this incremental phase-in model. Decisions beyond Grade 3 will rest on evolving research.

   A. Use results from year 1 to help plan year 2; use results from years 1 and 2 in planning year 3.
   B. Determine if projected and theory-based benefits actually accrue and factor these results into the planning: re-

duced retention in grade, increased achievement, parent involvement, early identification of students who need special services.

C. Think "out of the box" for creative uses of space to house small classes.

III. Plan long-range improvements throughout the system based on the small-class initiative. Study "trade-offs." Share results.

For example, if small classes reduce the number of students who require intensive remedial work, the teachers who formerly provided this remedial work—and their teaching spaces—can be reallocated to classes of 15:1. If timely remediation of early-identified problems that may lead to special education placement reduces the number of students needing special education, then.... If small classes reduce the number of youngsters retained in grade over several years, then.... If small classes bring increased involvement of parents who also will do some volunteer work, can they eventually replace a paid teacher aide or two?

Research, theory, and examples of good practice show that many benefits accompany small classes. Can they help pay for small classes? Not if everyone insists on "business as usual." A look out of the box might be salutary. Large-scale considerations of costs, personnel, and space may be daunting, but dividing these into "bite-sized" chunks may help put the problems in perspective. Incremental phasing in of small classes provides time and experience to guide future decisions. Case studies offer guidelines built from glimpses of success. Here are a couple examples.

In Success Starts Small or SSS (Achilles et al., 1994; Kiser-Kling, 1995), the two matched schools were in the same system: same curricula, per-pupil expenditures, etc. Flexibility generated mostly by schoolwide Title I eligibility of more than 70% of the children let one principal recommend small classes in Grades K–2. Effective use of resources and collaborative staff decisions effected class sizes of 15:1. Both schools had the same per-pupil expenditures; one school had 15:1 in K–2. The buildings did have space for extra classes—but a principal and faculty dedicated to 15:1 would have found alternatives if given the encouragement to try.

Other schools in North Carolina have implemented 15:1 with little or no increase in per-pupil expenditures. The entire Burke County, North Carolina, system has small classes in Grades 1–3. The Downtown Elementary School in Winston-Salem has small classes for preschoolers and Grades K–2. Per-pupil expenditures are the same there as in other elementary schools in the system that have larger classes. Berkeley County, South Carolina, and Fairfax County, Virginia, have small classes in "targeted" schools that have high percentages of at-risk children by purposeful distribution of special state and federal funds.

Much of the personnel cost and potential "shortage" in systems moving to 15:1 can be handled at the site level by staff planning and negotiations. A planning sheet developed by the principal to help in this decision process in Draper Elementary School, Rockingham County, North Carolina, appears as Table 9.1 of this text.

Because they are not in common practice, educators who wish to use small classes are on the edge of certainty about all of the benefits, trade-offs, and potential implementation processes. Research, theory, exemplary practice, and even traditional wisdom have contributed knowledge that small classes are important in education. The idea is not new. Educators, taxpayers, politicians, and policy people need the wisdom and will to use small classes well to obtain their beneficence.

The jury is in with a positive verdict on class size in education. Use of small classes is a leadership challenge. Plan ahead, but innovate enroute.

10

Class Size Does Matter

The study lasted for four years and, in my opinion, is the most significant educational research done in the US during the past 25 years.

(Orlich, 1991, p. 632)

Wisdom is not communicable ... Knowledge can be communicated, but not wisdom. One can find it, live it, be fortified by it, do wonders through it, but one cannot communicate and teach it.

(Hesse, 1951, p. 144)

Introduction

This chapter summarizes some points made in earlier chapters. Issues are presented as thoughts for policy, for use in schools, and for

added research. Modest speculation derived from combining the results of various studies is also advanced. At best, the material was
planned to communicate much of the knowledge derived about class
size in early primary grades that has been collected over the years.
The wisdom and the will to begin to redirect education's legacy of
neglect cannot be communicated. Educators, leaders, and parents
must decide to put kids first, finally. The decisions should be based
upon their collective wisdom that the investment in young people
is not only long overdue, it is appropriate and the duty of people of
integrity. Small classes for little students constitute education's IRA
(individual retirement account), invested at compound interest, in
environment-friendly securities.

Small Is Better; Less Is More

Energized by the Glass and Smith (1978) and Smith and Glass (1979)
meta-analyses and followed by some class-size interest and research
in the United States and Canada from about 1978–1982, it's taken approximately 20 years for class size to be taken seriously as a factor in
education. STAR results have taken about 10 years to have relatively
widespread consideration in policy decisions for American education. STAR and other carefully evaluated implementations of well-
designed small-class initiatives have shown a "class-size effect" that
includes a wide range of positive outcomes for students, teachers,
parents, and eventually for society at large.

The STAR, LBS, Challenge, and STAR Follow-up results have
been made widely available in many formats. Eventually, STAR findings attracted some attention, especially after reviews and positive
critical comments from respected researchers. STAR was a tightly
controlled, longitudinal experiment of class size that corrected for
many of the weaknesses identified in prior class-size studies. The
LBS, Challenge, and STAR Follow-up projects extended the STAR
experimental work. After his year-long review of the STAR studies,
Professor Emeritus Frederick Mosteller at Harvard commented that
experimental studies like STAR should provide a basis for education
policy and for changes in practice (1995):

> The Tennessee class size project, . . . illustrates the kind and mag-
> nitude of research needed in the field of education to strengthen

schools (p. 113). . . . It is important that both educators and policy makers have access to its statistical information and understand its implications. (p. 126).

Princeton economist and education production-function researcher Alan Krueger (1997, 1998) reanalyzed the K–3 STAR data, confirmed the original STAR findings, and extended those analyses in ways that could help leaders make policy decisions. Krueger's analysis supported the idea that positive outcomes could be obtained with only small differences in class sizes, in the range of 22–25 students, a class-size range of interest to persons doing large-scale (statewide) class-size changes such as in California. Krueger (1997, p. 27) added his voice to Mosteller's that STAR was an important study:

> One well-designed experiment should trump a phalanx of poorly controlled, imprecise observational studies based on uncertain statistical specifications.

Mosteller (1995) and Mosteller, Light, and Sachs (1996) argued forcefully that STAR and similar experiments should be used to inform educational policy decisions. Krueger (1997) explained why people should rely heavily on STAR results compared to earlier class-size studies, and why mixed results of some earlier class-size studies (or studies of PTR that were mislabeled as class-size studies) can be explained by reviewing them in light of STAR findings.

By 1999, approximately 38 states either had class-size legislation, had debated the topic seriously, had taken state board of education action, or had initiatives to test out class-size reduction in various conditions. Educators and policy persons in several foreign countries were considering or using class-size efforts to redesign their education systems. There has been some federal interest in class-size adjustments, especially in America's poorest schools. The President's 1998 proposed class-size initiative ran into roadblocks including political ideology; criticism from persons who mistake class size for pupil–teacher ratio, or who advocate other education changes. The facilities crisis brought about from (a) long-standing facilities neglect, (b) increasing enrollments, and (c) the move to smaller classes

with the mind-set that only classrooms in traditional school buildings will do for small groups of K–1 students looms to stop class-size
initiatives.

Some Contentiousness in Using Class-Size Results

Uses and proposed uses of STAR findings have generated predictable controversy in the public media and the professional literature, and among researchers, politicians, and policy people. In truc-
ulent tones reminiscent of Callahan's (1963) *Education and the Cult
of Efficiency*, some claim that there may be more efficient ways to improve student achievement or that it is expensive to reduce class size
in the early grades. This amazing assault on serious longitudinal,
replicable research is based on little but speculation—Shakespeare
might have said "sound and fury signifying nothing"—and questionable logic. For example, how can we really understand the "efficiency" of reducing class sizes until there are enough small-class activities around for long enough to allow the serious study of them?
Most dire cost predictions about the burden of small classes do
not factor in cost savings, long-term benefits, trade-offs, or systemic
changes that small classes may precipitate.

Class Size: Pervasive and Persuasive

Has any research shown harmful effects of small classes, or that
larger classes are better for children? How much success of some
popular projects and remedies might be attributed to a small-class
effect if the evaluations took class size into account as a separate variable? Are tutoring and cooperative learning really class-size treatments? Alternatives to regular public education thrive upon a small-
class effect: home schooling, alternative schools, charter schools,
private schools, apprenticeships, tutoring.

   The anti-class-size literature is replete with hypothetical discussions of how something else (we're not quite sure what that is or
how it might be done) *might* be a better or less expensive way to
get at the same academic and behavior outcomes achieved in small
classes. Favorite suggestions include spending the funds for technology, for incentives, for staff development, or for more projects.

Like the persistent visibility of small interest-group pressures in local districts, much of the anti-class-size noise comes from only a few
analyses that class-size critics cite incessantly and incorrectly.

Discussions about alternatives to class-size outcomes should
continue. However, we're just now beginning to understand the
long-term effects of early small-class education on later student behavior. *The STAR Follow-up Studies* (Pate-Bain et al., 1997) show long-
range outcomes in terms of education and social benefits, such as
drop-outs discipline actions, retention in grade, high school courses
of study, and grades achieved. Students in high school in 1996–
1997 who began school in STAR smaller rather than larger classes in
1985 had substantially better high-school outcomes: higher grades,
less retention in grade, etc. These results are similar to the long-
range outcomes of the Perry Preschool Program (Barnett, 1985, 1995;
Weikart, 1989, 1998; etc.). New policy research might review the
"trade-offs" in various class-size implementations, such as options
involving space use; social cost/benefit questions associated with
the high costs of retention, remediation, special education, student
indiscipline, etc. that small classes have been shown to ameliorate.
How might class size change influence many current education
practices?

Some Economic Questions Surrounding Class Size

Critical discussion and lively debates about class size, production functions, and cost–benefit in education have been initiated
by economists, policy persons, educators, and others (e.g., Burtless, 1996; Hanushek, 1995, 1996, 1998; Hedges & Greenwald, 1996;
Hedges, Laine, & Greenwald, 1994). Recent interest in the economics
of class-size processes and outcomes is evident in the work of Angrist and Lavy (1996), Boozer and Rouse (1995), Card and Krueger
(1996), Correa (1993), Krueger (1997, 1998), and Wenglinsky (1997).
Strangely missing here are the voices of teachers and of parents who
often express in surveys or polls their support of tax increases if the
funds will only go to improve education.

In future policy research, class-size issues might be connected
to space usage (proxemics) and the possibility that crowding little
children may contribute to later difficult behavior, such as the on-
set and nurturing of gangs in schools, or that large classes produce

stale air that adds to teacher fatigue and student inattentiveness late in the school day. How does early schooling in small classes extend recent findings of brain research, cognitive psychology, neuroscience, group dynamics, and community? Small classes increase student participation in and identification with school (Finn, 1989, 1993, 1998). If this leads to a positive trajectory of success in school and the probability that students will not drop out, does this support Lindsay's (1982, 1984) findings that school participation carries over into young adult participation in society? In the long term, might small classes reverse declining adult participation in government, at least in voting.

What are the implications of S for use of space, time, and technology in schooling? For improved school–home relationships? For innovative use of personnel?

As more answers become available about the benefits of small classes in education, definitive information about the efficiency of small class size should also become available. The STAR-generated class-size research has answered the question about the *effectiveness* of early small-class interventions that earlier meta-analyses uncovered. What should be the relationship between efficiency and effectiveness when we're talking about people, and particularly about the youngest people who are just beginning their long trek through our education system?

Bloom (1984a, 1984b) asked educators to seek answers to his "2-sigma problem" and "search for methods of group instruction as effective as one-to-one tutoring." The 2-sigma problem was to try to find some group-size instruction to match the outcomes of tutoring that could move a student approximately two standard deviations (2 sigmas) up the learning-outcome curve on standardized measures. Tutorials for every student in the public school system in every subject, however, would be impractical and extraordinarily expensive. How can educators approximate those learning outcomes in a group setting? Appropriately sized classes in K–3 are a start. They offer three socially desirable benefits that are expressed American values. Those benefits of quality, equality, and equity provide measurable positive outcomes and one mnemonic for education improvement:

improved education $= QE^2$. They also can be the basis for value-driven education leadership.

- *Quality.* Many indicators, including higher achievement in academics, behavior, citizenship, and development show the quality of small classes.
- *Equality.* All participants get the *same* treatment. No group gets more or less than another. Each student gets the same-sized scoop and flavor of ice cream.
- *Equity.* Minority and hard-to-teach youngsters benefit more from small classes than do other youngsters, but all benefit in a small class in positive ways. (Achilles, Finn, & Bain, 1997–98; Finn & Achilles, 1990; Robinson, 1990; Wenglinsky, 1997, etc.)

Improved education $= QE^2$: Small classes offer quality, equality, equity.

Class-Size Research Squares With Common Sense

One anomaly of class-size research is that for once, education research results parallel common sense so critics must assail people's collective traditional wisdom as well as the experimental evidence. Teachers know that they can teach better in small classes. Parents consistently ask that their youngsters be put into smaller classes. Parents get really involved in the school and classroom when the classes are small. Most projects and "treatments" for problem students rely on small classes or small numbers of "special" youngsters with a single teacher, so small classes for all children show that all children are special and provide overall school improvement. The often-espoused but seldom-employed "individualized" instruction idea actually becomes possible when a teacher has a manageable number of youngsters, and the teacher can be held accountable for student learning and achievement.

The class-size research raises many questions about early schooling, but the use of small classes also generates problems that require serious work. Besides the PTR–class size discussion, educators may need now to consider space vs. classrooms, use of remote or satellite primary-grade centers connected by technology to a home-based school, reassignment or redeployment of some educators, and alternate ways to prepare teachers. Small classes raise issues of space and crowding, and subsequent or resultant student behaviors. Small classes intersect with the continuing emphasis on school size as an important schooling variable. In addition to the stand-alone benefits of small classes, class size and the *effective school correlates* fit well together, and this mutual support is reassuring.

Table 10.1 shows the effective school correlates with selected outcomes of small classes. Small classes in the early primary grades get an effective school off to a head start. Some similarities between effective schools and class-size outcomes are shown in Table 10.1 and discussed here.

- *Emphasis on and acquisition of basic skills*. Teachers in small classes report that the students complete the lessons in less time than do students in larger classes, leaving time to teach for mastery. Test results show that students in small classes outperform students in large classes on both standardized and criterion-referenced tests.

- *High expectations for students and others in the school*. Teacher morale and intrinsic rewards from positive student outcomes lead to high expectations that students will succeed. Teachers believe that they can help students learn more in small classes, and administrators and others expect students and teachers to do well in small classes.

- *Frequent monitoring of student progress*. Teachers report being able to read with each child daily and hear each child respond or recite in the small class. Teachers use alternative forms of assessing student learning.

- *A positive climate conductive to learning*. With fewer children in a class, there is more space per child and there are more materials, toys, and places for learning centers. This reduces student and teacher stress and student indiscipline; it improves student personal relations, group dynamics, and student–teacher interaction.

- *Sufficient opportunity for learning*. Small classes increase student time on task, allow teachers to use a variety of centers to activate multiple intelligences, increase the numbers of learning

TABLE 10.1 Sample of Selected Small-class Research Outcomes That Support the *Effective School Correlates*[a]

Effective School Correlate	Small-Class Outcome
1. Acquisition of basic skills	Students in small classes, K–3 get .3 to .7 effect size (ES) test-score gains over students in larger classes on test scores.
2. High expectations	Teachers express high morale and describe student success.
3. Frequent monitoring of progress	Teachers read with each child each day. Individual work identifies and remediates problems. Students don't fall behind. Teachers know when students reach mastery.
4. A positive climate for learning	Less crowding, more sharing, fewer disruptions and discipline referrals; more materials per student
5. Sufficient opportunity for learning	Increased time on task and one-on-one time with teacher; decreased classroom management problems. More space for learning centers
6. Parental and community involvement on a partnership basis	Increased parent involvement, volunteer efforts, attendance at school events (PTA, open house, etc.); opportunities for partnerships, such as employment-based early primary spaces
7. Strong school leadership	Not directly measured. The small-class effort requires creative and strong leadership.

[a] *Effective Schools Report* (Dynamic Educational Information, Inc., 1997).

materials/books available for each child, and make it possible for teachers to employ the good teaching practices that they know about but that large classes had hindered them from using.

- *Parent and community involvement.* Research has shown that small classes bring with them an increase in parent involvement and interest in schooling. School administrators report increased support for and confidence in schools when there are small classes. Teachers can get to know each student's family.
- *Strong school leadership.* The class-size research has not yet provided specific results about this effective school correlate. Anecdotal evidence points to the need for leadership to solve problems: innovative approaches to scheduling, to finding spaces for small classes; alternative use of staff. At the district level, especially, small classes provide many opportunities for leaders to exercise creativity to solve problems related to space, finding certified teachers, reporting to parents and the media, etc.

There are many valid parallels between small-class benefits and the effective schools correlates. If the effective schools correlates make sense and have helped improve schooling, it should surprise no one to find connections between them and class-size elements.

Teacher Aides: A Policy Conundrum

STAR's in-school design could as easily make STAR an experimental study of teacher-aide effects as a study of class-size effects. The emphasis on class size has overshadowed the teacher aide question that has not yet been fully examined by STAR researchers. Achilles et al. (1993c) questioned sub-par performance of the teacher-aide classes in STAR. Boyd-Zaharias and Bain (1998) compiled *Teacher Aides and Student Learning, Lessons From Project STAR* for Educational Research Service, but much analysis of aide effects remains to be done. The STAR data seem to show that of the three STAR conditions, the small class (S) was best, generally followed by the regular class (R) and then by the regular class with a full-time aide (RA). This experimental finding may help explain mixed results obtained in Prime Time where a teacher aide could be used to change the student-to- adult ratio in lieu of establishing a second class (Chase, Mueller, & Walden, 1986; Tillitski et al., 1988).

STAR was not the first study to show that aides did not help student outcomes (e.g., Davidson, Beckett & Peddicord, 1994). Macro-level evidence on teacher-aide effects is contained in the generally poor results obtained by Title I over the years (Abt Associates, 1997; Borman & D'Agostino, 1996; Wong & Meyer, 1998). Besides Prime Time, the Nevada class-size initiative is getting mixed results. Because of space limits, one class-size treatment in Nevada is two teachers in a large class of students. The inevitable conclusion from combining these results is that *class size, not PTR or teacher aides, influences student outcomes.*

The teacher-aide findings present serious policy problems. Teacher aides constitute a large population of education workers. Use of teacher aides is an employment and economic, as well as an education, issue. Many teachers rely on teacher aides. Teacher aides often live in the immediate community served by the school and know the community and the people there; the teachers may commute. As demography and education practice change, teacher aides may be important in assisting a teacher with inclusion—the placement of students needing special treatment in the regular classroom rather than in resource rooms or self-contained settings. Teacher aides may be indispensable in helping teachers with bilingual or English as a Second Language (ESL) and limited English proficiency (LEP) students and in helping teachers understand the cultures of students from the community.

Yet, using teacher aides where they are not absolutely indispensable for the sorts of reasons stated above is to support employment and job generation with funds that could be used to reduce class sizes and increase benefits to students. The efficient and effective use of teacher aides is an area begging for more solid research.

Class Size and Safety

School safety has been illuminated in the harsh glare of some shocking violence. School violence, although deplorable, may be also overstated. According to the American Association of School Administrators (1998, p. 5),

1. Violence is a societal issue, not merely a school issue. You cannot have islands of safety in a sea of community violence. . . . Children in America die of gun deaths at about 12 times the rate of other countries. Is it any wonder some die in school?
2. Schools are the safest place for students to be. Each year, more than 3,000 children die of handgun wounds in the United

States. About 1% of these fatalities occur in school. The other
99% happen at home or in the street.

Federal interest in school safety and some funding have followed the national goal of achieving safe and drug-free schools.

Class-size research shows that outcomes associated with small
classes (and with small schools) are the foundations of safe schools:
improved student behavior and human relations skills; increased
participation in schooling and school-sanctioned events; increased
sense of community and family in small classes; and a generally improved school climate where teachers, students, and parents feel less
stress than in larger classes and larger schools. Smallness promotes
knowledge of individuals that can head off violence before it happens. Although much connects the use of small classes and schools
to positive student behavior, much research remains to be done here.
The research needs to be long range, and can only be done as small
classes become available for the research. The analogy, however, to
the use of small classes in successful alternative schools for difficult
youth is a powerful guideline. Class size and school size are administratively mutable variables.

Schoolwide Remedial Projects

Given the presence of a class-size effect and the competing costs of
some schoolwide remedial projects such as the popular and useful
Success for All (SFA), serious analyses might determine what portion
of some projects can be attributed simply to use of small classes to get
their gains. If special projects provide little benefit for their costs over
and above what could be gained by schoolwide class-size reduction,
the schoolwide initiative should be small classes. Projects might help
the few especially difficult and needy students who require even
more direct individual attention than a small class can allow.

Fashola and Slavin (1998, p. 376) found that only three of the 13
schoolwide reform models they studied met their evaluation criteria for achievement, and two of these three were Slavin's own models. Strangely missing from that analysis were two other very carefully evaluated models: Reading Recovery and small classes. (Both
of these efforts have long and careful implementations and very positive evaluations.) All three models that meet the evaluation crite-

ria use small classes. What part of their effect is left over for the "model"?

Most remedial projects used in schools today are expensive. Some were developed with federal funds—tax dollars. Levin (1998, p. 9) made the following observation:

> In fact, I believe that they ought to be made available at low cost and question why they are sold commercially at high prices, given the substantial grants and subsides provided for their development by government agencies ... presumably to reduce costs and promote their use.

Projects that rely on class-size effects to get their positive results drive the project-mentality, "pull-out" or "add-on" approach to education that hinders the full-scale use of small classes. To the extent that these projects use both pull-out and teacher-aide treatments, the class-size effect may have lots to overcome! The "add-on" and teacher-aide processes have grown in popularity since Title I and have not been seriously evaluated except as part of Title I over the years. Class size *has* been seriously researched and found to work. Class-size research helps address the Miles and Darling-Hammond (1998, p. 9) concern that "very little research addresses how schools might organize teaching resources more effectively at the school level." Research on redeployment of teaching resources should include the use of teacher aides, especially if aides are major components of special projects.

Student and Teacher Interactions and Benefits

Success Starts Small (Achilles et al., 1994; Kiser-Kling, 1995) offered an opportunity to study teacher behaviors in small classes. Three of the four teachers who had the small classes (15:1) in Grade 1 began their teaching careers in those small classes. Except for student teaching in "regular" classes, they did not have experience teaching in larger classes. A cynic might say that they had not yet developed bad habits from years of teaching hordes of children in cramped spaces. The principal who chose to use Title I funds for class sizes of about 15:1 in first grade instead of for the traditional "pull-out" programs interviewed the teachers as a group after their first year of small-class teaching. The following are summarized responses of the four first-grade teachers to their principal's (Jean Owen, Ed.D.) questions about their students. A few teacher-narrated anecdotes about teaching in small classes follow the summarized responses. The answers and the anecdotes offer a snapshot of the benefits to students and teacher that occur in small classes.

Questions About Reading, Mathematics, and Acceptable Behaviors

1. "How many of your students are reading?" 42 or 84% are reading (of the 8 not reading, 3 are being assessed for EMH self-contained, 3 for LD, and 2 seem to be emerging as readers).
2. "How many of your students can do math?" 44 or 88%
3. "How many students were referred for severe discipline problems?" 3 or 6%
4. "If you had a regular class size of 24 to 28 students, how many of your students might develop severe discipline problems?" 19 or 38%
5. "If you had a regular class size of 24 to 28 students, how many of your students might be referred to special classes?" 8 or 16% (8 is the enrollment of many self-contained classes)

The Teachers Offered Anecdotes About Their Children

☺ If I had 28 students as I did in my practice teaching, and had them all in rows, I could not accommodate the 5 very low-functioning children. As it is, they may go to a self-contained classroom as second graders (when they no longer have the small-class option). But in the meantime, I can see that they are learning; they see themselves as successful, vital persons in our class. Other students assist them in doing their work.

☺ In this (15:1) situation, not only do I know the students very well, they know each other very well. They know who can do what—who can help spell a word, who can read, who has been sick and with what. Quotes from students: "I'll bet Heather can read that hard book. Dericas is sick. Do you know what is wrong with him? I dropped by Dericass' house and saw him, and he really is sick." When Anthony came back after several days of sickness, they all cheered that he was back.

☺ Some of my children who haven't started to read yet, want to read and do "pretend reading." Their classmates patiently and knowingly accept that and help them with their pretend reading. They move the marker or tell them the words.

☺ The troubled children who need a lot of attention from me get that attention. With the 24 students I had in my practice teaching, I would not have had the time to give that attention, so the students would have begun to act out and become discipline problems. I have the time and the relaxation to give the attention to the child who needs a minute or so more without worrying about losing the other children and the class.

☺ I feel like I am being a successful teacher to all the students.

☺ I really know where my children are in their learning because I can ask them how they figured something out. I can focus on each of them and diagnose just how they learn.

☺ With the five very low students in my small class, I have time to try different ideas to help them. With 24 students, I'd have time to try one or two and they might not work, so the child would probably be referred out of class.

☺ I had enough unifix cubes for each student to work with 100 cubes when we studied the concept of 100.

Use Research: Class Size, Not PTR, Should Be a Policy Base

Policy decisions and evaluations of education outcomes need to be made separately for class size and for PTR. Mingling class size and

PTR results causes confusion, blunts the positive impact of class size, and hides shortcomings associated with PTR.

The hesitation of leaders to advocate small classes and the tortuous approach to understanding the power of small classes have been driven by uncritical acceptance and substitution of PTR results as class-size outcomes. People who have developed reputations in policy circles by arguing that class size does not matter based upon analyses of PTR and PTR outcomes are understandably reluctant to support small classes now. Consider the sound and fury that have been raised about class-size benefits based on discussions of PTR outcomes!

"Class-size reduction" at least suggests that some rational, extant research-based class size is in general use. After Bloom's (1984a, 1984b) pioneering work, the current research on class size is providing the first serious look at what class sizes might be needed today so educators can meet the challenges of the changing contexts and demographics of education's clients.

Federal Policy Trends:
Small Classes Are Good Policy and Good Politics

The federal policy debate about class size may be shifting slightly toward smaller classes. Tomlinson (1998, p. 37), *Class Size and Public Policy: Politics and Panaceas*, summarized the federal policy position as follows:

> Evidence to date ... does not generally support a policy of limiting class size in order to raise student achievement or to improve the quality of work-life for teachers; nor does it justify small reductions in pupil/teacher ratios or class size on order to enhance student achievement. Research also fails to support school policies designed to lower class size if these do not first specify which pupils will benefit and how and why they will do so. [Note the class-size–PTR confusion.]

By 1997, the U.S. Department of Education's report (1997, p. 29) *Building Knowledge for a Nation of Learners*, included the statement that "studies ... such as reducing class size in the primary grades, have proved to help children get a good start in school." This report was followed in 1998, ten years after the Tomlinson report, by *Reducing Class Size: What Do We Know?* (Pritchard, 1998, p. 14), which included the following statement:

> Reducing class size to below 20 students leads to higher student achievement. However, class-size reduction represents a considerable commitment of funds, and its implementation can have a sizable impact on the availability of qualified teachers. . . . There is more than one way to implement class-size reduction, and more than one way to teach in a smaller class. Depending on how it's done, the benefits of class-size reduction will be larger or smaller.

In a 1998 U.S. Department of Education-commissioned report, Finn (1998, p. 13) concluded that "a clear small-class advantage was found for inner-city, urban, suburban, and rural schools; for males and females; and for white and minority students alike" and that there is lots of room for added research to address lingering issues and questions. There won't be much class-size research until there are ample small classes for researchers to study.

The shift in emphasis on class size by the U. S. Department of Education may be based on newer class-size studies, but the class-size position reflects political agendas of the times. The total amount of federal funding for education is minor when compared to local and state support, so efforts to get manageable-sized classes for young children need to target state and local policymakers more than federal officials. Second, federal education funding is primarily categorical, directed to specific groups or for single purposes, such as special education, bilingual education, vocational education, or at-risk students. Funding for class-size reduction as discussed here is general or across-the-board so that all students in the grades affected would benefit. An approach to using small classes that makes sense when funds are limited would be to target class-size reductions to schools or even to classes that have high densities of students whom smaller classes have been shown to help more. Wenglinsky (1997, pp. 24, 25)) summarized thus: "In other words, fourth graders in smaller-than-average classes are about a half a year ahead of fourth graders in larger-than-average classes ... The largest effects seem to be for poor students in high-cost areas."

Unfortunately, the federal position as stated by Pritchard (1998, p. 14) seems to suggest just adding funds, not redesigning an education system creaky with neglect and poor habits. Good policy and good politics might see class-size change as the foundation for major education overhauls.

A Caveat About "Standardized" Comparisons and Class Size

Small classes make a difference in student achievement in early grades. The differences are most easily shown by comparisons of student outcomes in smaller classes with outcomes of students in larger classes, *especially* on standardized or normed indicators. As smaller classes become the norm in early education, student performance will increase, but now that all students are performing at higher levels, the standardized tests will be normed upward, for *not* to do so would realize the Lake Wobegon desideratum "where all the children are above average." Once again, adults will have pushed children to higher levels of performance and then, through statistical manipulation, found reason to complain that half of the students in U.S. schools are below average, U.S. schools are subpar, teachers are low quality, and public education costs too much. The fault is not so much with education, educators, and children as with the measurement processes used to gauge education and in the misunderstanding of the value, use, and meaning of standardized tests. Small classes can only do so much. People must understand that if small classes become widely used, the complaint about lack of student performance will likely be a complaint about a higher level of performance than before small classes became prevalent. Students may benefit, but now they may have to run even faster just to stay even.

In Conclusion

If we've not had really serious discussions on class size issues and implications before, at least let's get serious about a research-driven base for major policy shifts in American education. We have knowledge about one scientifically validated way to improve early schooling for children. Small K–3 classes offer quality, equality, and equity.

How to do what research shows should be done is a fair question for enlightened policy discussions, political decisions, educational leadership, and a new series of education studies. These positive steps will require a collective national wisdom. Time's a-wasting.

> Dateline May, 1997. Anne Lewis reported that Marshall Smith, acting deputy secretary in the U.S. Department of Education told an AERA audience in Chicago (3/97) that "We know kids can learn at much higher levels if we give them more opportunities to learn."
>
> *Lewis* (1997), *78* (9), p. 671

I don't know what the acting deputy secretary knew then, but I do know that small classes in K–3 provide the students "more opportunities to learn." When what to do is known, how to do it should take precedence. Let's try!

Let's Get on With a Better Way

American education has been suffering a legacy of neglect from tax abatements, media attacks, and unrealistic comparisons to outcomes in other nations, to declining facilities, class-size-increase creep, inattention to research results, policies that result in unfunded liabilities, faddism, political and polemic pronouncements (ad nauseam). There must be a better way to conduct the business of education, but beset by so many special interests and negativism, education is much like the Edward Bear we meet on the very first page of *Winnie the Pooh*.

> Here is Edward Bear, coming downstairs now, bump, bump, bump, on the back of his head, behind Christopher Robin. It is, as far as he knows, the only way of coming downstairs, but sometimes he feels that there really is another way, if only he could stop bumping for a moment and think of it. And then he feels that perhaps there isn't.
>
> (Milne, 1926, p. 1)

Resource A:
Abbreviations
and Glossary

Burke County The locally funded use and study of small classes in Burke County, North Carolina, to improve student outcomes in Grades 1–3. Results have been outstanding and local support continues.

Challenge A policy implementation of STAR's experimental findings in 16 poor counties with low-performing schools. Results were successful in terms of student test-score gains.

Class size The number of students regularly in a teacher's room and those for whom that teacher is responsible and accountable. Class size can be determined by counting the number of students in a teacher's class. Class size can be set experimentally, as in Project STAR, but even there researchers used a range, such as 13–17 for a small class.

In-School Design The research model employed in STAR in which any participating school had at least one of each of the three class-size conditions as a way to control for district and building-level variables. The powerful design was parsimonious and guaranteed that the control group would not suffer attrition.

LBS	Lasting Benefits Study "tracked" STAR students in Grades 4–8 by their class type in Grades K–3 to examine the continuing class-size effect.
Pupil–Teacher Ratio (PTR)	A number manufactured by dividing the number of students at a site (e.g., a building) by the number of professionals serving that site (sometimes includes instructional aides). According to Cahen and Filby (1979, p. 492), "the search for an appropriate descriptive ratio has a long history in the research on class size. Any ratio is, at best a crude indicator. . . ." The accuracy of any PTR will greatly influence the results of any studies that use the ratio as one variable. Note that in STAR, the range for small classes was set at 13–17 to 1 teacher, but PTRs for these small classes were the same as the PTR for the building. Even though the class sizes were different, the PTR for both small and regular classes was the same at the building level.
Regular Class (R)	A class size ranging from 22–26 students set experimentally and randomly to be the "control" condition in STAR. The R classes in STAR averaged about 25:1.
Regular-Aide Class (RA)	A regular class (22–26) in STAR that also had a full-time teacher aide. The RA condition was the second experimental condition in STAR.
SAGE	Student Achievement Guarantee in Education is a closely monitored class-size effort in selected Wisconsin schools. Initial results are similar to STAR outcomes (Molnar, 1998).
Small Class (S)	For practical purposes, and considering current legislation and practice, a "small" class has about 15–18 students per teacher and is designated in this book as 15:1 or 18:1.
SSS	Success Starts Small, a year-long observational study of teacher behaviors in small (14:1) and regular (25:1) classes in schools matched on many variables (Achilles et al., 1994).
STAR	Student Teacher Achievement Ratio, a longitudinal class-size experiment (1985–1989) conducted in Tennessee. The study eventually included more than 11,600 students. STAR provided experimental evidence to support prior meta-analyses and studies (Word et al., 1990).

Resource B: Effect Sizes of Class "Drift"

(This section is adapted from Finn and Achilles [1998]. Work was supported in part by a grant from the Spencer Foundation titled "A Study of Class Size and At-Risk Students.")

As this book was being prepared, several STAR researchers continued to analyze STAR data. One key effort is to understand not only the immediate K–3 results, but the long-term benefits of small classes in elementary grades. Researchers are reanalyzing the data to determine the actual effect sizes (ESs) of the statistically significant differences between small (S) and the other class types, regular (R) and regular with an aide (RA).

In these analyses, each ES is the difference between the average of the S and the average of the two other class types combined, divided by the standard deviation of the R classes. The ESs for criterion-referenced tests are differences in the percentages of students passing the tests.

The original ESs *underestimated* the true effects of STAR differences. In Grades 1, 2, and 3, some classes "drifted" out of range because of mobility, etc. Table B.1 shows the drift "out-of-range" by years. The ESs will be greater if the "out-of-range" classes, the sections marked "B" on Table B.1, were removed.

TABLE B.1 Distribution of STAR Classes by Grade (K–3) by Designations S (Small), R (Regular), and RA (Regular and Aide), Showing "Drift" From the Experimental Range[a]

		K (n classes)			1 (n classes)			2 (n classes)			3 (n classes)		
		S	R	RA	S	R	RA	S	R	RA	S	R	RA
B	11										2		
	12	8			2			3			2		
A	13	19			14			16			15		
	14	22			18			27			17		
	15	23		1	31			32			31		
	16	31	4		16	1		29	1		31		1
	17	24	4	1	33	1		19			27		
B	18		1	2	6	2		6			10	1	
	19		7	6	3	4	3	1	3	3	5		4
	20		6	6	1	10	6		2	1		9	13
	21		14	12		18	18		7	11		11	12

(continued)

TABLE B.1 Continued

	K (n classes)			1 (n classes)			2 (n classes)			3 (n classes)		
	S	R	RA	S	R	RA	S	R	RA	S	R	RA
22		20	20		27	15		23	21		13	16
23		16	21		19	20		20	21		10	14
C 24		19	14		16	11		22	25		15	14
25		6	6		7	9		9	15		116	15
26		4	3		5	9		6	7		5	12
27		1	6		2	4		4	1		5	8
B 28			1		1	2		1	0		2	6
29					1	2		2	2		2	2
30					1	1						
TOT n	127	99	99	124	115	100	133	100	107	140	90	107
%	40	30	30	37	34	29	39	29	32	41	27	32
N	325			339			340			337		

[a] A = range for S; B = "out of range"; C = range for both R and RA classes. These numbers represent the students who took a test; classes could have been larger, but not smaller. Of particular concern are classes in the 18–21 range.

Furthermore, differences in ESs over time may be more appropriately represented by grade equivalents (GEs) that are based on developmental scales rather than on test publishers' item-response theory scales devised to have the same standard deviation in each grade (Hoover, 1984). (For a comparison of status scores with developmental scores, see Hoover [1984].)

In computing the GEs (still in progress), the continuing and cumulative benefits of an early small-class start in schooling are made very clear. For example, using just the Total Reading results in STAR, the (S) advantage in months of schooling (the average GE of the [S] minus the average GE of [R] students) *increases* from .8 in kindergarten, to 1.7 and 2.7 in Grades 1 and 2, and to 5.8 in Grade 7. Results obtained by Pate-Bain et al. (1997) in the *STAR Follow-up Studies* and analyses in process by Bain and colleagues show increasing academic and social benefits that accrue to S students into high school.

References

Abt Associates (1997). *Prospects*. Bethesda, MD: Author.

Achilles, C. M. (1996). *Summary of recent class-size research with an emphasis on Tennessee's Project STAR and its derivative research studies.* Nashville, Tennessee State University.

Achilles, C. M., Finn, J. D., & Bain, H. P. (1997-1998). National Association of Secondary School Principals (1995). *Breaking Ranks.* Alexandria, VA: Author.

Achilles, C. M., Harman, P., & Egelson, P. (1995). Using research results on class size to improve pupil achievement outcomes. *Research in the Schools, 2*(2), 23-30. (Paper by same title presented at AASA convention, 2/95.)

Achilles, C. M., Kiser-Kling, K., Owen, J., & Aust, A. (1994). *Success starts small: Life in a small class.* (Final Report. Small-Grant/School-Based Research Project). Greensboro: University of North Carolina at Greensboro. (ERIC EA 029049)

Achilles, C. M., Nye, B. A., & Bain, H. P. (1994-1995). The test-score "value" of kindergarten for pupils in three class conditions at grades 1, 2, and 3. *National Forum of Educational Administration and Supervision Journal, 12*(1), 3-15.

Achilles, C. M., Nye, B. A., Bain, H. P., Zaharias, J. B., & Fulton, B. D. (1993, November). *The teacher aide puzzle: Student achievement is-*

sues. *An exploratory study.* Paper presented at the Mid-South Educational Research Association (MSERA) meeting, New Orleans, LA.

Achilles, C. M., Nye, B. A., Zaharias, J. B., & Fulton, B. D. (1995, April). *Policy use of research results: Tennessee's Project Challenge.* Paper presented at the American Educational Research Association meeting, San Francisco, CA.

Achilles, C. M., Nye, B. A., Zaharias, J. B., Fulton, B. D., & Cain, V. (1996, March). *The continuing and cumulative contribution of long-term cooperative research on schooling: Executive summary.* Paper presented at the American Association of School Administrators meeting, San Diego, CA.

Achilles, C. M., & Price, W. J. (1999). Can your district afford smaller classes in grades K–3? Can smaller classes be cost effective? *School Business Affairs, 65*(1), 10-16.

Achilles, C. M., Sharp, M., & Nye, B. (1998, March). *Attempting to understand the class size and pupil–teacher ratio (PTR) confusion: A pilot study.* Paper presented at the AASA conference within a convention, San Diego, CA. (ERIC EA 092051)

Akerhielm, K. (1995). Does class size matter? *Economics of Education Review, 14*(3), 229-241.

Allen, Y. (1998, April). Class size: Smaller is better. President's perspective. *National Association of Elementary School Principals Communicator, 2.*

American Association of School Administrators (1998). Five points to make about school violence. *Leadership News, 1*(3), 5.

Angrist, J. D., & Lavy, V. (1996, July). *Using Maimonides' rule to estimate the effect of class size on children's academic achievement.* Mt. Scopus, Jerusalem: Hebrew University.

Bach, R. (1997). *Jonathan Livingston Seagull.* MacMillan

Bain, H., Achilles, C. M., Dennis, B., Parks, M., & Hooper, R. (1988). Class size reduction in metro-Nashville: A three-year cohort study. *ERS Spectrum, 6,* 30-36.

Bain, H. P., Achilles, C. M., McKenna, B., & Zaharias, J. (1992). Class size does make a difference. *Phi Delta Kappa, 74*(3), 253-256.

Bain, H. P., Achilles, C. M., & Witherspoon-Parks, M. (1988, November), *Three-year longitudinal study of small class size: The metro-Nashville Public Schools Study: 1984–1987.* Paper presented at the Annual Conference of the Mid-South Educational Research Association (MSERA), New Orleans, LA.

Barnett, W. S. (1985). Benefit–cost analysis of the Perry preschool program and its policy implications. *Educational Evaluation and Policy Analysis, 7*(4), 333-342.

Barnett, W. S. (1995). Long-term effects of early childhood programs on cognitive and school outcomes. *The Future of Children: Long-Term Outcomes of Early Childhood Programs, 5*(3), 25-48.

Bingham, S. (1993). *White-minority achievement-gap reduction and small class size: A research and literature review.* Nashville, TN: Tennessee State University, Center of Excellence for Research in Basic Skills.

Bingham, S. (1994). *White-minority achievement-gap reduction and small class size: A research and literature review.* Nashville, TN: Tennessee State University, Center of Excellence for Research in Basic Skills.

Bloom, B. S. (1984a). The search for methods of group instruction as effective as one-to-one tutoring. *Educational Leadership, 41*(8), 4-17.

Bloom, B. S. (1984b). The 2-sigma problem: The search for methods of group instruction as effective as one-to-one tutoring. *Educational Researcher, 13*(6), 4-16.

Boozer, M., & Rouse, C. (1995, May). *Intraschool variation in class size: Patterns and implications* (Paper 344; ED 385935). Princeton, NJ: Princeton University, Industrial Relations Section.

Borman, G. D., & D'Agostino, J. V. (1996). Title I and student achievement: A meta-analysis of federal evaluation results. *Educational Evaluation and Policy Analysis, 18*(4), 309-326.

Boyd-Zaharias, J., Achilles, C. M., Nye, B. A., & Cain, V. A. (1994). Random class assignment and student achievement; A Project STAR ancillary study. In E. Chance (Ed.), *Creating the quality school* (pp. 367-379). Madison, WI: Magna.

Boyd-Zaharias, J., Achilles, C. M., Nye, B. A., & Fulton, B. D. (1995). Quality schools build on a quality start. In E. Chance (Ed.), *Creating the quality school* (pp. 116-123). Madison, WI: Magna.

Boyd-Zaharias, J., & Pate-Bain, H. (1998). *Teacher aides and student learning: Lessons from Project STAR.* Arlington, VA: Educational Research Service.

Burke County (NC) Public Schools. (1992, July). *Reduced class size: Pilot project.* Morganton, NC: Author.

Burke County (NC) Public Schools. (1993). *Reduced class size: Grades 1 and 2.* Morganton, NC: Author.

Burke County (NC) Public Schools. (1998, June). *Reduced class size: A summary of results, 1992-1993 through 1997-1998.* Morganton, NC: Author.

Burtless, G. (1996). Introduction and summary. In G. Burtless (Ed.), *Does money matter?* (pp. 4-42). Washington, DC: Brookings Institution.

Byrd, R. S., Weitzman, M., & Auinger, P. (1997). Increased behavior problems associated with delayed school entry and delayed school progress. *Pediatrics, 100*(4), 654-661.

Cahen, L. S., & Filby, N. (1979). The class size/achievement issue: New evidence and a research plan. *Phi Delta Kappa,* 492-495, 538.

Cahen, L. S., Filby, N., McCutcheon, G., & Kyle, D. W. (1983). *Class size and instruction.* White Plains, NY: Longman.

Calhoun, J. B. (1962). Population density and social pathology. *Scientific American, 206*(2).

Callahan, R. (1963). *Education and the cult of efficiency.* Chicago, IL: University of Chicago Press.

Card, D., & Krueger, A. B. (1996). Labor market effects of school quality: Theory and evidence. In G. Burtless (Ed.), *Does money matter?* (pp. 97-140). Washington, DC: Brookings Institution.

Casey, A. E. (1998). *Kids count data book.* Baltimore, MD: Annie E. Casey Foundation.

Cavenaugh, R. (1994). Class size and best practice. *Education Alternatives, 3*(1), 3.

Chase, C. I., Mueller, D. J., & Walden, J. D. (1986, December). *Prime Time: Its impact on instruction and achievement* (Final Report). Indianapolis: Indiana Department of Education.

Clinton, W. (1998, January 28). State of the Union address. *New York Times,* p. 19A.

Cooley, W. W. (1993, May). *The difficulty of the educational task* (Paper 16). Pittsburgh, PA: University of Pittsburgh, Pennsylvania Educational Policy Studies.

Cooper, H. B. (1989a). Does reducing student-to-instructor ratios affect achievement? *Educational Psychologist, 24*(1), 79-98.

Cooper, H. B. (1989b, November). Synthesis of research on homework. *Educational Leadership, 46*(3), 85-91.

Correa, H. (1993). An economic analysis of class size and achievement in education. *Education Economics, 1*(2), 129-135.

Cotton, K. (1996). *School size, school climate, and student performance* (Close-up 20). Portland, OR: Northwest Regional Laboratory.

Darling-Hammond, L. (1998). Teachers and teaching: Testing policy hypotheses from a national commission report. *Educational Researcher, 27*(1), 5-15.

Davidson, C. W., Beckett, F. E., & Peddicord, H. Q. (1994). *The effects of a statewide teacher aide program on functional literacy examination scores of eleventh-grade students.* Paper presented at the Mid-South Educational Research Association meeting, Nashville, TN.

Dynamic Educational Information, Inc. (1997, August). The seven correlates of an effective school. *Effective Schools Report, 15*(7).

Educational Research Service (1980). *Class size research: A critique of a recent meta-analysis*. Arlington, VA: Author.

Egelson, P., Harman, P., & Achilles, C. M. (1996). *Does class size make a difference?* Greensboro, NC: Southeastern Regional Vision for Education (SERVE).

Ellis, T. I. (1984). *Class size: A digest prepared for ERIC-CEM*. Eugene, OR: ERIC-CEM.

ERIC-CEM. (1994). *Value search: Class size*. Eugene, OR: Clearinghouse in Educational Management.

Evertson, C. M., & Folger, J. K. (1989, March). *Small class, large class: What do teachers do differently?* Paper presented at the American Educational Research Association meeting, San Francisco, CA.

Evertson, C. M., & Randolph, C. H. (1989). Teaching practices and class size: A new look at an old issue. *Peabody Journal of Education, 67*(1), 85-105.

Fairfax County (VA) Schools. (1997, July). *Evaluation of the reduced-ratio program* (Final Report). Fairfax, VA: Office of Program Evaluation, Fairfax County Schools. (J. DiStefano, principal investigator)

Fashola, O. S., & Slavin, R. E. (1998). Schoolwide reform models: What works? *Phi Delta Kappa, 79*(5), 370-379.

Filby, N., Cahen, L., McCutheon, G. & Kyle, D. (1980). *What happens in smaller classes?* San Francisco, CA: Far West Laboratory for Educational Research. (ERIC ED 219 365)

Finn, C. E., Jr. (1997, October 29). The real teacher crisis. *Education Week, 48*, 36.

Finn, J. D. (1989). Withdrawing from school. *Review of Educational Research, 59*(5), 117-142.

Finn, J. D. (1993, August). *School engagement and students at risk*. Washington, DC: National Center for Educational Statistics, U.S. Department of Education. (NCES 93-470)

Finn, J. D. (1998, April). *Class size and students at risk: What is known? What is next?* Washington, DC: U.S. Department of Education. Office of Educational Research and Improvement. (AR 98 7104)

Finn, J. D., & Achilles, C. M. (1998, October). Paper presented at the Northeast Educational Research Association meeting, Ellenville, NY.

Finn, J. D., & Achilles, C. M. (1990). Answers and questions about class size: A statewide experiment. *American Educational Research Journal, 27*(3), 557-577.

Finn, J. D., & Achilles, C. M. (1998, April). *Tennessee's class-size study: Questions answered, questions posed.* Paper presented at the American Educational Research Association annual meeting, San Diego, CA.

Finn, J. D., Achilles, C. M., Bain, H. P., Folger, J. Johnston, J., Lintz, M. N., & Word, E. (1990). Three years in a small class. *Teaching and Teacher Education, 6*(2), 127-136.

Finn, J. D., & Cox, D. (1992). Participation and withdrawal among fourth-grade pupils. *American Educational Research Journal, 29*(1), 141-162.

Finn, J. D., Fulton, D., Zaharias, J., & Nye, B. (1989). Carry-over effects of small classes. *Peabody Journal of Education, 67*(1), 75-84.

Finn, C. E. Jr., & Petrilli, M. J. (1998, March 9). The elixir of class size. *The Weekly Standard, 3*(25), 16-18.

Fowler, W. J., & Walberg, H. J. (1991). School size, characteristics, and outcomes. *Educational Evaluation and Policy Analysis, 12*(2), 189-202.

French, R. L., & Galloway, C. M. (nd). *Communication events: A new look at classroom interactions* (Mimeo paper). Knoxville: University of Tennessee.

Glass, G. V., Cahen, L. S., Smith, M. L., & Filby, N. (1982). *School class size: Research and policy.* Beverly Hills, CA: Sage.

Glass, G. V., & Smith, M. L. (1978). *Meta-analysis of research on the relationship of class size and achievement.* San Francisco: Far West Laboratory for Educational Research and Development.

Glickman, C. (1991). Pretending not to know what we know. *Educational Leadership, 48*(8), 4-10.

Hall, E. T. (1966). *The hidden dimension.* Garden City, NY: Doubleday.

Hall, E. T. (1976). *Beyond culture.* Garden City, NY: Doubleday.

Hamburg, D. A. (1992). *Today's children.* New York: Time Books, Random House.

Haney, D. Q. (1998, September 28). At 50, heart study keeps fingers on nation's pulse. *USA Today*, p. 5D.

Hansel, S. (1997). *Worksheet: Conversion of current staffing into options for class-size adjustments.* Eden, NC: Draper Elementary School, Rockingham County, NC Schools.

Hanushek, E. A. (1995). Moving beyond spending fetishes. *Educational Leadership, 53*(3), 60-64.

Hanushek, E. A. (1996). School resources and students' performance. In G. Burtless (Ed.), *Does money matter?* (pp. 43-73). Washington, DC: Brookings Institution.

Hanushek, E. A. (1998, February). *The evidence on class size.* Rochester, NY: The University of Rochester, W. Allen Wallis Institute.

Harvey, B. (1993, December). *An analysis of grade retention for pupils in K–3.* Unpublished doctoral dissertation, University of North Carolina, Greensboro. (This dissertation extends the STAR, LBS, and Challenge data as a way to try to understand the impact of either a small class or a full-time teacher aide on the conditions being studied.)

Harvey, B. (1994). *Retention: A narrative review of one hundred years of practice. What are the alternatives?* Nashville, TN: Tennessee State University, Center of Excellence for Research in Basic Skills.

Hayden, J., with K. Cauthen. (1996). *Children in America's schools* (portions narrated by Bill Moyers). Corporation for Public Broadcasting, a co-production of the Saint/Hayden Co. and South Carolina ETV.

Hedges, L. W., & Greenwald, R. (1996). Have times changes? The relationship between school resources and student performance. In G. Burtless (Ed.), *Does money matter?* (pp. 74-92). Washington, DC: Brookings Institution.

Hedges, L. W., Laine, R. D., & Greenwald, R. (1994). Does money matter? A meta-analysis of studies of the effects of differential school inputs on student outcomes. *Educational Researcher, 23*(3), 5-14.

Herzberg, F. (1966). *Work and the nature of man.* Cleveland, OH: World Publishing.

Hesse, H. (1951). *Siddhartha.* (H. Rosner, Trans.). New York: New Directions.

Hibbs, B. F. (1997). *Relationships among discipline factors and early student placement in small (1:15), regular (1:25) and regular-with aide classes.* Unpublished doctoral dissertation, University of North Carolina, Greensboro.

Hodgkinson, H. (1985). *All one system.* Washington, DC: Institute for Educational Leadership.

Hodgkinson, H. (1991). Reform vs. reality. *Phi Delta Kappa, 73*(1), 8-16.

Hodgkinson, H. (1992). *A demographic look at tomorrow.* Washington, DC: Institute for Educational Leadership.

Hodgkinson, H. (1995, October). What should we call people? Race, class, and the census for 2000. *Phi Delta Kappa, 77*(2), 173-179.

Hoff, D. J. (1998, October 7). Scholars seek new solutions to the "achievement gap." *Education Week,* p. 5.

Holmes, C. T. (1989). Grade-level retention effects: A meta-analysis of research studies. In L. A. Shepard and M. L. Smith (Eds.), *Flunking grades: Research and policies on retention* (pp. 16-23). New York: Falmer.

Holmes, C. T., & Matthews, K. M. (1984). The effects of nonpromotion on elementary and junior high school pupils: A meta-analysis. *Review of Educational Research, 54,* 225-236.

Hoover, H. D. (1984). The most appropriate scores for measuring educational development in the elementary schools: GE's. *Educational Measurement: Issues and Practice, 3,* 8-14.

Johnston, J. M. (1990). *What are teacher's perceptions of teaching in different classroom contexts?* Paper presented at the American Educational Research Association meeting. Boston, MA.

Jung, C. (1964). Approaching the unconscious. In C. Jung et al. (Eds.), *Man and his symbols.* Garden City, NY: Doubleday.

Kiser-Kling, K. (1995). *A comparative study of life in first grade classrooms of 1:14 and 1:23 teacher pupil ratios (sic. Really class size).* Unpublished doctoral dissertation, the University of North Carolina at Greensboro.

Kozol, J. (1992). *Savage inequalities.* New York: Harper Collins.

Krueger, A. B. (1997, June). *Experimental estimates of education production functions* (National Bureau of Economic research paper 6051). Princeton, NJ: Princeton University.

Krueger, A. B. (1998, January). Reassessing the view that American schools are broken. *Federal Reserve Bank of New York Economic Policy Review,* 29-43.

Levin, H. M. (1998). Educational performance standards and the economy. *Educational Researcher, 27*(4), 4-10.

Lewis, A. (1997, May). Washington commentary. *Phi Delta Kappa, 78*(9), 671.

Lewit, E. M., & Baker, L. S. (1997). Class size. *The Future of Children: Financing Schools, 7*(3), 112-121.

Lindbloom, D. H. (1970). *Class size as it affects instructional procedures and educational outcomes.* ERIC Document ED 059 532

Lindsay, P. (1982). The effect of high school size on student participation, satisfaction, and attendance. *Educational Evaluation and Policy Analysis, 4*(1), 57-65.

Lindsay, P. (1984). High school size, participation in activities, and young adult social participation: Some enduring effects of schooling. *Educational Evaluation and Policy Analysis, 6*(1), 73-83.

Martini, S. (1994). *Undue influence.* New York: Jove Books.

McPartland, J., Jordon, W., Legters, N., & Balfanz, R. (1997). Finding safety in small numbers. *Educational Leadership, 55*(2), 14-17.

McRobbie, J., Finn, J. D., & Harman, P. (1998, August). *Class size reduction: Lessons learned from experience* (Policy Brief 23). San Francisco, CA: West Ed.

Miles, K. H. (1995). Freeing resources for improving schools: A case study of teacher allocation in Boston public schools. *Educational Evaluation and Policy Analysis, 17*(4), 476-493.

Miles, K. H., & Darling-Hammond, L. (1998). Rethinking the allocation of teaching resources: Some lessons from high-performing schools. *Educational Evaluation and Policy Analysis, 20*(1), 9-29.

Milne, A. A. (1926). *Winnie-the-Pooh.* New York: E. P. Dutton.

Molnar, A. (1998). *Smaller classes, not vouchers, increase student achievement.* Harrisburg, PA: Keystone Research Center.

Mosteller, F. (1995). The Tennessee study of class size in the early school grades. *The Future of Children, 5*(2), 113-127.

Mosteller, F., Light, R. J., & Sachs, J. A. (1996). Sustained inquiry in education: Lessons from skill grouping and class size. *Harvard Educational Review, 66*(4), 797-828.

Mueller, D. J., Chase, C. I., & Walden, J. D. (1988). Effects of reduced class sizes in primary classes. *Educational Leadership, 45,* 48-50.

Nye, B. A., Achilles, C. M., Boyd-Zaharias, J., Fulton, B. D., & Wallenhorst, M. (1994). Small is far better. *Research in the Schools, 1*(1), 9-20.

Nye, K. (1995, August). *The effect of school size and the interaction of school size and class type on selected student achievement measures in Tennessee elementary schools.* Unpublished doctoral dissertation, University of Tennessee, Knoxville.

Olson, M. N. (1971). Research notes—Ways to achieve quality in school classrooms: Some definitive answers. *Phi Delta Kappa, 65.*

Orlich, D. (1991). Brown v. Board of Education: A time for a reassessment. *Phi Delta Kappa, 72*(8), 631-632.

Pate-Bain, H. P., Zaharias, J. B., Cain, V. A., Word, E., & Binkley, M. E. (1997, September). *STAR follow-up studies, 1996–1997.* Lebanon, TN: HEROS, Inc.

Pritchard, I. (1998, May). *Reducing class size: What do we know?* (OERI SI 98-3027). Washington, DC: U.S. Department of Education.

Robinson, G. L. (1990). Synthesis of research on the effects of class size. *Educational Leadership, 47*(7), 80-90.

Shapson, S. M., Wright, E. N., Eason, G., & Fitzgerald, J. (1980). An experimental study of the effects of class size. *American Educational Research Journal, 17,* 141-152.

Shepard, L. A., & Smith, M. L. (1990). Synthesis of research on grade retention. *Educational Leadership, 49*(8), 84-88.

Shulman, L. (1988). Disciplines of inquiry in education: An overview. In R. Jaeger (Ed.), *Contemporary methods for research in education* (pp. 3-20). Washington, DC: American Educational Research Association.

Smith, M. L., & Glass, G. V. (1979). *Relationship of class-size to classroom processes, teacher satisfaction and pupil affect: A meta-analysis.* San Francisco, CA: Far West Laboratory for Educational Research and Development.

Snyder, T., & Achilles, C. M. (1996-1997). Will "triage" be education's next metaphor? *National Forum of Educational Administration and Supervision, 13*(3), 25-33.

Steinberg, L., Brown, B., & Dornbusch, S. M. (1996). *Beyond the classroom: Why school reform has failed and what parents need to do.* New York: Simon & Schuster.

Tillitski, C., Gilman, D., Mohr, A., & Stone, W. (1988). Class size reduction in North Gibson School Corporation: A three-year cohort study. *ERS Spectrum, 6*(4), 37-40.

Tinbergen, N. (1952, December). The curious behavior of the stickleback. *Scientific American, 187*(6).

Tomlinson, T. M. (1988, March). *Class size and public policy: Politics and panaceas.* Washington, DC: U.S. Department of Education, Office of Educational Research and Improvement. (PIP 88-838)

U.S. Department of Education. (1997). *Building knowledge for a nation of learners.* Washington, DC: Author.

Voelkl, K. (1995). *Identification with school.* Unpublished doctoral dissertation, State University of New York, Buffalo. (UMI 0538143)

Weikart, D. P. (1989, June). *Quality preschool programs: A long-term social investment* (Occasional Paper 5). New York: The Ford Foundation School Welfare and the American Future.

Weikart, D. P. (1998, July 8). High scope study raises direct-instruction questions. Commentary. *Education Week, 17*(42), 46.

Weld, J. (1998, June 3). Beyond the salary carrot. *Education Week, 17*(38), 33.

Wenglinsky, H. (1997). *When money matters.* Princeton, NJ: Educational Testing Services, Policy Information Center.

Whittington, E. H., Bain, H. P., & Achilles, C. M. (1985). Effects of class size on first-grade students. *ERS Spectrum, 3*(4), 33-39.

Wong, K. K., & Meyer, S. J. (1998). Title I schoolwide programs: A synthesis of findings from recent evaluation. *Education Evaluation and Policy Analysis, 20*(2), 115-136.

Word, E., Johnston, J., Bain, H., Fulton, B., Zaharias, J., Lintz, N., Achilles, C. M., Folger, J., & Breda, C. (1990). *Student/teacher achievement ratio (STAR): Tennessee's K-3 class size study.* Final report and final report summary. Nashville, TN: Tennessee State Department of Education.

Zaharias, J. B. (1993, December). *The effects of random class assignment on elementary students' reading and mathematics achievement.*

Unpublished doctoral dissertation, Tennessee State University, Nashville. (This dissertation extends the STAR, LBS, and Challenge data as a way to try to understand the impact of a small class on the conditions being studied.)

Zaharias, J. B., Achilles, C. M., & Cain, V. A. (1995). The effect of random class assignment on elementary students' reading and mathematics achievement. *Research in the Schools, 2*(2), 7-14.

Zaharias, J. B., Achilles, C. M., Nye, B. A., & Cain, V. A. (1995). Random class assignment and student achievement: A Project STAR ancillary study. In E. Chance (Ed.), *Creating the quality school* (pp. 367-379). Madison, WI: Magna Publishers.

Suggested Readings

Achilles, C. M. (1988, April). *If not before, at least now.* Paper presented at the American Educational Research Association annual meeting, San Diego, CA. (ERIC EA 029052)

Achilles, C. M. (1996). Students achieve more in smaller classes: A response to Hanushek. *Educational Leadership, 53*(5), 76-77.

Achilles, C. M. (1997). Small classes: Big possibilities. *The School Administrator, 54*(9), 6-15.

Achilles, C. M. (1998, February). *Class-size research supports what we all know. (So, why aren't we doing it?).* Paper presented at the American Association of School Administrators annual meeting, San Diego, CA. (ERIC EA 029050)

Achilles, C. M., Nye, B. A., Zaharias, J. B., & Fulton, B. D. (1993, January). *The Lasting Benefits Study (LBS) in Grades 4 and 5: A legacy from Tennessee's four-year (K–3) class-size study (1985–1989), Project STAR.* Paper presented at the North Carolina Association for Research in Education (NCARE) meeting, Greensboro, NC.

Achilles, C. M., Nye, B. A., Boyd-Zaharias, J., & Fulton, D. B. (1993). Creating successful schools for all children: A proven step. *Journal of School Leadership, 3*(6), 606-621.

Bracey, G. (1998). The eighth annual Bracey report on the condition of education. *Phi Delta Kappa, 80*(2), 112-131.

French, N. K. (1993). Elementary teacher stress and class size. *Journal of Research and Development in Education, 26*(2), 66-73.

Greenwald, R., Laine, R. D., & Hedges, L. W. (1996). The school funding controversy: Reality bites. *Education-Leadership, 53*(5), 78-79.

Johnson, R. C. (1997a, April 30). New one-on-one time helps teacher uncover well-hidden learning problems. *Education Week, 16*(29), 39.

Johnson, R. C. (1997b, April 30). Class-size cuts in Calif. bring growing pains. 1, 38.

Kohn, A. (1998). Only for *my* kid. *Phi Delta Kappa, 78*(8), 569-577.

LeTendre, H. M. (1991). Improving Chapter 1 programs: We can do better. *Phi Delta Kappa, 72*(4), 577-580.

Madden, N. A., Slavin, R. E, Karweit, N. L., Dolan, L. J., & Wasik, B. A. (1993). Success for all: Longitudinal effects of a restructuring program for inner-city elementary schools. *American Educational Research Journal, 30*(1), 123-148.

Natriello, G., McDill, E., & Pallas, A. (1990). *Schooling disadvantaged children: Racing against catastrophe.* New York, NY: Teachers College Press.

Pallas, A.M., Natriello, G., & McDill, E. L. (1995). Changing students/changing needs. In I. Flaxman & H. Passow (Eds.), *Changing populations: Changing schools, NSSE, Part II* (pp. 30-58). Chicago IL: University of Chicago Press.

Reynolds, A. J. (1992). Grade retention and school adjustment: An exploratory analysis. *Educational Evaluation and Policy Analysis, 14*(2), 101-121.

Shepard, L. A., & Smith, M. L. (1989). *Flunking grades: Research and policies on retention.* New York: Falmer.

Slavin, R. E. (1996, December). Reforming state and federal policies to support adoption of proven practices. *Educational Research, 25*(9), 4-5.

Texas Education Agency. (1992). *Acceleration vs. remediation and the impact of retention in grade on student achievement.* Austin, TX: Author.

Tomlinson, T. M. (1990). Class size and public policy: The plot thickens. *Contemporary Education, 62*(1), 17-23.

U.S. Department of Education. (1996, July). *Pocket projections of education statistics to 2006* (OERI/NCES 96-660). Washington, DC: Author.

U.S. Department of Education. (1997). *Teachers' working conditions.* (OERI/NCES 97-371). Washington, DC: Author.

Annotated Bibliography

Achilles, C. M. (1996). *Summary of recent class-size research with an emphasis on Tennessee's project STAR and its derivative research studies.* Nashville: Tennessee State University, Center of Excellence for Research on Basic Skills, 56 pages. This summary primarily emphasizes Project STAR and the series of class-size studies closely connected to STAR or studies conducted by STAR-related personnel. The author raises selected social and political considerations and possible research topics to increase the understanding of class-size outcomes. The publication includes an extensive bibliography.

Boyd-Zaharias, J., & Pate-Bain, H. (1998). *Teacher aides and student learnings: Lessons from Project STAR.* Arlington, VA: Educational Research Service (ERS), 31 pages. This "relevant research for school decisions" document explains general STAR findings and specific outcomes of STAR's second experimental condition, the use of a full-time instructional aide. Zaharias and Bain conclude that STAR results did not support the use of full-time aides to increase student achievement.

Egelson, P., Harman, P., & Achilles, C. M. (1996). *Does class size make a difference?* Greensboro, NC: Southeastern Regional Vision for Education (SERVE), Regional Education Laboratory, 40 pages.

191

The Regional Laboratory report of recent class-size interest in North Carolina warns readers to make careful distinctions between class size and pupil–teacher ratio (PTR). The report contains highly readable summaries of state-level class-size initiatives and emphasizes the positive outcomes of locally supported class size reduction in Burke County in Grades 1–3.

Finn, J. D. (1998, April). *Class size and students at risk: What is known? What is next?* Washington, DC: U.S. Department of Education, Office of Educational Research and Improvement (AR 98–7104), 38 pages. This easily read and carefully presented review of class-size studies includes priorities for added research and questions why the persistent class-size effect may exist. The document summarizes research on academic effects of small class size, assessing costs and benefits of smaller classes, and instructional practice and student behavior. The report emphasizes Project STAR.

Krueger, A. B. (1998, January). Reassessing the view that American schools are broken. *Federal Reserve Bank of New York Economic Policy Review,* 29–43. Using production-function and economic analyses, Krueger analyzes school outputs such as test-score change over time. A major portion reports on a reanalysis of STAR outcomes that shows continuing growth over time and a class-size effect within the control group.

Molnar, A. (1998). *Smaller classes, not vouchers, increase student achievement.* Harrisburg, PA: Keystone Research Center, 48 pages. In this clearly written report, Molnar contrasts the Milwaukee Parental Choice Voucher Program with Wisconsin's Student Achievement Guarantee in Education (SAGE) outcomes and shows how SAGE results "track" with STAR and STAR-related studies.

Mosteller, F. (1995). The Tennessee study of class size in the early school grades. *The Future of Children: Critical Issues for Children and Youths,* 5(2), 113-127. Mosteller's clear and cogent review brought the STAR Project to public attention and energized the recent class-size debates. Mosteller critically analyzes the strengths and weaknesses of STAR, discusses the effect sizes of the results, and puts class size into perspective as education policy. Highly recommended.

Mosteller, F., Light, R. J., & Sachs, J. A. (1996). Sustained inquiry in education: Lessons from skill grouping and class size. *Harvard Educational Review,* 66(4), 797-827. Three scholars analyze two long-term topics of educational concern that also have extensive research legacies. They identify the good studies, major themes, and the outcomes that deserve consideration in education policy and planning. The section on class size provides analyses of STAR and STAR-related studies.

Pate-Bain, H., Boyd-Zaharias, J., Cain V., Word, E., & Binkley, M. E. (1997). *STAR follow-up studies, 1996–1997*. Lebanon, TN: HEROS, Inc. Based on a limited sample of Grade 11 students who had been in STAR in Grades K–3, the authors identify long-term results that seem related to small-class early schooling. Some benefits include higher grades in high school, fewer retentions and dropouts, selection of college-preparatory courses such as calculus and foreign language, and fewer suspensions from school. This pilot study showed ways to locate students and conduct follow-up studies using the STAR database.

Index

CORWIN
PRESS

The Corwin Press logo — a raven striding across an open book— represents the happy union of courage and learning. We are a professional-level publisher of books and journals for K–12 educators, and we are committed to creating and providing resources that embody these qualities. Corwin's motto is "Success for All Learners."